Hints for Personal Success

I0169509

About the Author

Karel de Laat completed his bachelor's and master's degrees in psychology and his doctorate in history in Australia. He has worked as an organizational psychologist for forty years, specializing in organization and career development. During this time he featured in newspapers and on radio, providing practical advice on how to achieve personal and business success, as well as presenting seminars on a wide range of business and career development subjects. In his spare time, Karel served in the Australian Naval Reserve for thirty years, attaining the rank of Rear-Admiral. He now devotes his time to mentoring, consulting, public speaking and writing.

About the Book

Hints for Personal Success is full of examples of how to use the experience of others to make your life more rewarding. Psychologist Karel de Laat has provided advice to owners and managers of large businesses and to their many employees. In his work, he collected numerous anecdotes and used them to motivate and guide his clients. Karel believes that everyone has a unique role to play in the world, focusing on those with whom we live, work and relax. We can all experience life to the full, even though we do not get the same publicity as the people we may see presented to us in the media every day. The key to realizing our personal success is taking control of our lives, not living in the shadow of public opinion. Karel's anecdotes show in a practical way how each of us can achieve the personal success we want, or make the dramatic step to realizing we already have it right in front of us, but just have not been able to see or grasp it yet.

Readers' Comments

'Your book of insights is both extensive and concise and full of good advice.'

Senior Manager, Strategy and Risk Management

'The book is helping me identify so many of the personalities that you talk about. It has helped me calm down and identify that a lot of the issues here are not mine and I need to just keep positive and do my job to the best of my ability.'

Administrations Supervisor

'Do read this book; it will show you how to walk tall, stand your ground, keep your eye on the ball, deflect those arrows and most importantly to stand confidently in the sunshine knowing your shadow will harm no one.'

Teacher and writer

'Working in the community sector with people with disabilities requires a range of skills, but the most important skill is to recognise a person's ability and help them believe in themselves to achieve their goals. I have used Karel's philosophy on personal success, not only to achieve my goals, but to help many others achieve theirs. Hints for Personal Success delivers a message to anyone that reads it, but more importantly helps you develop your own philosophy and values to achieve your personal success in your own way.'

Community Sector Employment Consultant

'Hints for Personal Success is the Lonely Planet guide for finding your way through life.'

Senior IT Professional

Published by:
de Laat & Co
PO Box 9 Ferny Hills Distribution Center
Brisbane QLD Australia 4055
www.delaatco.com

The preferred citation for this book is

FK de Laat, *Hints for Personal Success*, de Laat & Co, Brisbane, 2014.

Author: Karel de Laat
Title: Hints for Personal Success/Karel de Laat
ISBN: 978-0-9872878-0-9
Subjects: psychology, philosophy

Hints

for

PERSONAL

SUCCESS

Karel de Laat

'The manner in which one single ray of light, one single precious hint, will clarify and energize the whole mental life of him who receives it, is among the most wonderful and heavenly of intellectual phenomena'.

Arnold Bennett[1]

'**positive psychology** *n*. The psychology of valued psychological phenomena, such as contentment and satisfaction (with the past), hope and optimism (for the future) and happiness and well-being (in the present).[2]

Contents

Preface

'Hints for Personal Success' featured on radio for some years as a short burst of advice about practical ways to deal with life's personal challenges. I was often asked to publish a compilation of my scripts, but just never found the time. Essentially these are 'opinion pieces' that were a quick bit of infotainment, so they are designed to be applied in your daily routine if you think they would work for you.

The aim was to provide a bit of food for thought based on the principle that being positive and constructive in your day to day life could make you a bit more successful. Also, people used to say 'I know him' or 'I have worked there', but the situations are generally based on a whole series of experiences that have resulted in a case study based on no single event. Mostly, I tested the ideas while working with people I coached through personal or work-related challenges, using the simple scenarios to present thoughts and options for approaching different situations.

Well here it is! I hope you find the ideas useful in this format and that they can help you find a bit more personal success. Basically, the book is a general reader with each segment illustrating one independent idea, so I have published them in alphabetical order by title, but the index provides more information on how to find particular subjects within the many of the topics discussed.

Karel de Laat

Introduction

They say beauty is in the eye of the beholder, well so is personal success. This book is all about your personal success. No one can decide whether you are successful, except you.

The stories in this book are based on my experiences with people just like all of us. We are all seeking to live a happy and fulfilled life. The only trouble is we all have times when we get confused about what that means.

I hope that by reading these examples you understand that you are not alone in trying to find personal success. In particular, I hope that you will learn that personal success is something you can get a little more of each day, just by being aware that the opportunity is there.

Everybody has ups and downs. How you manage these inevitable day to day changes determines how happy you will be. As with managing anything, preparation is critical.

If you accept that there will always be a need to prepare yourself for what life is going to bring your way, you will have made an important first step in finding personal success.

Essentially, the stories in this book talk about being positive to give yourself the best possible chance of managing situations well. They suggest that a high level of personal commitment and integrity is essential in order to be truly successful.

In addition, there are examples of how being your own person plays a key role in finding happiness and stories that give examples about how caring for others is an essential part of finding contentment.

I hope that some of these hints make it into your personal success lifestyle and make you more content with what life offers each day.

Hints for Personal Success

Ability to cope with adversity

Coaching a person who was having difficulty finding employment helped reinforce for me that the ability to cope with adversity is a key factor in being successful.

In this case, although under a lot of pressure, the candidate was seeking the widest possible range of alternatives to minimize the effect of these problems on him and his family.

The ability to cope with adversity by taking a positive approach is not just a function of your personality. You can use the goal-directed skills of visualizing your goals and writing down your strategies to help you cope with adverse circumstances.

In these tough pressure situations it can be extremely difficult, but you should aim to clear your mind of feelings of fear and panic to allow constructive thinking to prevail.

Using relaxation techniques can help with clearing the mind and some people practice techniques like yoga and tai chi to help them achieve peak performance as well as a back-up for the tough times.

Just like these techniques, strategies that have helped you succeed in the past should be on the top of your list for possible solutions in the tough times. In very severe circumstances, it may be advisable to seek counseling or even medical intervention to allow you to relax.

The most important issue is that you remain in control of the circumstances, as much as you can, and direct all activities towards a goal that is predetermined by you.

Even though your hold on the rudder may be a little shaky, it is important to remember that success will often come more easily if you can maintain an approach that has served you well in the past.

Act now

One characteristic of people who are successful is that they can act immediately when a situation demands it.

Complex words like procrastination are in common use for a very good reason. Everybody procrastinates in some way. Many people delay and think and ponder until, by the time they act, it is far too late.

It is not that successful people act without thinking. On the contrary, they analyze, choose a course of action and then act quickly and decisively. The aim is to strike the perfect balance between the two sayings 'They who hesitate are lost' and 'Look before you leap'.

The truly successful person just seems to develop a better feel for where to go and how to get there in time to 'Strike while the iron is hot'.

Developing this decisive style is not done by magic. It comes about through not closing down your systems when problems arise, but remaining alert and attacking problems vigorously.

However, that does not mean going at it 'Like a bull at a gate' (sorry about all the clichés, but people just seem to remember things that are really familiar and it helps to make the point), it means to get started (with a good plan) – now.

The aim is to not run away from your next problem, but to attack it head on. In this way, you will find the solution will come to you much more quickly, because you have discovered the real problem or challenge, not the one the fear planted in your mind.

As always, you will find the secret of success is constant practice. You will have to invest a fair amount of time, but the pay-off will be worth the effort.

Actions speak louder than words

In implementing a performance improvement program for a football team, it became evident that actions truly do speak louder than words.

This program involved visualization training to improve on field performance. After the training, if someone was still unable to or could not pick the gaps to run into there was no pretending that the mental training program had worked for them.

This can be a very embarrassing test of one's ability as a trainer but can also provide tremendous rewards.

This is because visible success in a sport is much more dramatic than behavioral changes, with the latter being very much a matter of personal opinion.

An important part of being successful is realizing that demonstrable achievement is a key factor in any success story. Everyone should be looking for success that cannot be disputed.

It is probably because of this type of clarity that accumulation of wealth is so often regarded as an indicator of success.

In a similar way, sporting achievement is so much a part of creating society's heroes, because these achievements are seen and judged by the spectators using the same rules of - 'look at the scoreboard'.

In striving for personal success, there is certainly considerable merit in finding an area where achievement is judged fairly and is clearly visible to all.

Look around, I think you will find that putting yourself to the test is tough, but has its rewards.

Approach each day with a fresh outlook

Successful people approach each day with a fresh outlook. They leave their problems from yesterday behind them.

If they have a bad day, successful people do not harbor the thought that it is the beginning of an unhealthy trend.

I do not think there would be anybody who has not had at least one bad day and we have probably all had more than our fair share at different times.

The trick to being successful lies in realizing that most days can be very positive, if you decide that you can have an impact on just how many of them are going to be positive.

You do this by maintaining your belief that a fresh approach to each day puts the odds in your favor.

The key to having this positive mental outlook each day is realizing that the word outlook refers to a forward plan not a rear guard analysis.

Concentrating on what will be and not what has been is merely habit and can be very profitably combined with a strategy of guiding the day rather than letting it guide you.

I am not suggesting that you forget the importance of learning from experience and using that for future preparation, strategy, and so on, or leaving fate to the wind.

Rather, you should add to your planning and implementation actions the strong sense that a new day means new opportunities.

So as each day comes, look forward, think positive and leave any negative experiences in the past where they belong.

Avoid the 'Meanies'

It is always sad to meet with someone who confirms that there are people out there in your world who are just outright mean.

However, it is a fact of life that the bell curve is alive and well and there are just as many really mean people as there are really nice people.

Unfortunately, when one of the mean people gets into a position where they can influence the lives of many others, there is not normally a lot that can be done about it by the people who are most under threat.

This is one of those few occasions where I have to support the strategy of beating a hasty retreat. If you cannot change the situation, suffering is definitely not a recipe for success.

You are far better advised to move on and find another situation where the people that you work with, or for, are human beings who create an atmosphere of pleasure, achievement and overall success in a team environment.

So do not hesitate, if you get caught in this type of situation, to make the move elsewhere. Do not feel that you have to be a martyr and suffer it. If you have to move on, put all of your energies into finding a suitable alternative. Remember personal success is not always about winning battles, it is about enjoying the challenges of life.

As so many people have said, 'life is a journey not a destination' and the company you keep is a key part of that journey. You need to remember that a big part of personal success planning is making sure you never end up working with or for the 'meanies' of the world.

Learn to identify the 'meanies' and you will be able to avoid them and make your path to personal success a pleasure. Having the opportunity to make a choice is the first part of this process, exercising the opportunity is the second.

Be an individual

Many so called 'preachers' of success recommend particular avenues for achieving your goals.

Very often they suggest that you should follow very set guidelines that leave you no room to engage in any free thinking or erratic behavior.

In my view, it is very important to remember that you are an individual and that if we eliminated the individual behavior out of the path to success, many geniuses would never have contributed some of the greatest ideas and inventions that the world has seen.

So, while setting of goals and careful planning for their achievement is a vital part of success, you should never ignore your creative side and the need for letting the spirit run free with a good idea.

All of this goes to reinforce the view that we are all individuals and should maintain our individuality no matter what system we adopt for finding success, but using a good plan to get there remains a key success strategy.

So look inside yourself and do not let systems take over the part of you that makes you unique. Your uniqueness is vital to your well being and success in life.

Just for fun, why not write down the things about you that make you unique. I will leave the space blank (no lines) so you can write, squiggle, draw, or do what takes your fancy.

Be aware of different perspectives

One very important lesson for all of us is acquiring an awareness of the different perspectives held by other people.

It is very common to make the mistake of believing that other people view the world exactly as we do, particularly in areas such as honesty, reliability and so on.

There are a wide range of perspectives and approaches to other people that do not fall outside the law, but are certainly at the less desirable end of the spectrum. You need to be aware that they exist and not get caught out.

But remember, someone who adopts a successful approach to life does not take these different perspectives to heart and become bitter.

You should be aware, however, that your perspective on honesty, reliability and similar characteristics, that form that essence of self called 'good character', is not necessarily shared by each and every individual that you meet.

The key to being successful is keeping this clearly in mind, dealing with people on their merits, making your own decision about how a person's perspective fits with your own (or not) and then making decisions about potential personal or working relationships accordingly.

Without developing a cynical view about having to sit constantly in judgment upon others, it is very advisable on the trail to success to ensure early on that you are dealing with people who are like minded rather than those who will cause you grief by maintaining and acting upon beliefs that you are not happy with.

Be competitive

There is a lot of talk these days about everybody working in a team situation and sharing the glory, the responsibility and the authority.

This is all well and good, but if you are very underlined individually competitive, do not be put off.

Individual competition and strong personal motivation has been the reasons behind many major outstanding achievements over the centuries.

What is important is that the individual is in the situation where these characteristics are needed and appreciated.

A team player in a highly individually competitive environment may not do well, just as a highly individually competitive person might not do well in a team environment. For this reason, it is important to know your particular style and to find the environment where that style is most successful.

Matching your strengths to the circumstances in sport, work or just day to day life activities is a real skill.

The saying about square pegs not going into round holes illustrates how it is the match between you and the environment that is important, not just your profile.

Get the best fit for your ambitions and personal style and you will do well.

So, what is your style? Why not put a few thoughts here.

Be convinced

One of the essential elements of introducing a positive approach to life is to be convinced that it will actually work. Some people actually approach the process of being positive with a negative attitude. It is no wonder there is no result.

It is essential that you remain totally convinced that being positive in every way is sufficient to get you a positive result about feeling good about life.

I use the happiness in - happiness out philosophy because it gives you such a good understanding about the process of feeding yourself positive inputs to get positive outputs. For example, if you do not feed in anything negative, nothing negative can come out the other side unless you introduce it yourself.

In the same way, if you are super busy introducing positives and blocking the entry of any negatives, you will be so busy you won't have time to introduce any negatives. This is why you see athletes with their eyes, ears and minds glued to their chosen input before a big event.

In the final analysis, you have got to be convinced that being positive and working on a 'happiness in - happiness out' philosophy will work. Plus, you have got to be convincing in talking to other people about it. In fact, being convincing in talking to other people about your philosophy is one of the key blocking strategies to prevent negativity coming into your system.

So there it is, 'happiness in' equals 'happiness out'. All you have to do is turn your back on the garbage in, garbage out philosophy which pervades many peoples' lives. That really isn't that hard to do if you realize that a lot of what comes your way and that you accept without any scrutiny, is garbage. So, say no to garbage, say yes to happiness in, and happiness out will work for you.

Be cordial

Having an encounter with a service technician very recently made me realize once again how important it is to maintain a cordial approach in your dealings with other people.

This particular person was clearly not comfortable with his role and, when difficulties arose, he moved quickly to being defensive and to attacking others verbally when it was just not appropriate.

To be cordial does not mean to be subservient. It means to remain polite no matter how firm you may need to be in delivering unpleasant news, about the failure of a product and the cost of the repair, for example.

In fact, the cordiality associated with maintaining a level head can be just that much more dramatic in its impact when contrasted with the possibly very negative message that is being delivered.

The really successful people that I recall most, based on their ability to have a really positive personal impact, were able to keep their cool, never lost respect for the other person and practiced cordiality even when the circumstances were grim and the solutions being implemented were harsh.

Sometimes this personal impact can be that much greater when it occurs after you have had an initial bad experience, as happened to me recently.

In this case, the person who picked up the pieces, after her colleagues, in person and by phone, had dropped the ball badly was one of the most professional, and cordial, people I have met.

Opinions in this area will differ, but my view is that emotionality resulting in verbal abuse or any other form of nasty behavior is just not appropriate and not at all associated with individual personal success. Cordial people, on the other hand, are winners.

Be friendly

As I was coming off the golf course recently I was giving the great Australian salute by waving some flies away from my face. Suddenly, I noticed two people in a car waving happily to me as they drove out of the golf club.

Just as a natural reaction I waved back at them thinking they were waving at me. Only moments later did I realize that they were waving at me because they had interpreted my great Australian salute as a cheery greeting.

This incident made me think how important it is to be naturally open and friendly. The success that comes from a friendly open style is not usually associated with the achievement of any external goal, but it can contribute so much to the achievement of your own personal goals in your interactions with other human beings.

The tradition of waving to someone you see on a country road is something that has sadly disappeared long ago amongst city people. In fact, things have deteriorated to the point where people are suspicious of your sanity or your motives if you greet them and they have not met you before.

Nevertheless, I like to think that the feeling of belonging and warmness that a friendly smile or wave creates has not disappeared and that it is something that can be experienced by all of us if we are a little more friendly and liberal with our greetings.

For your part, just a little more friendliness can make you much more personally contented and you may be pleasantly surprised at some of the outcomes in terms of other peoples' behavior.

Be genuine (Part One)

I recall vividly having my first meeting with the Chief Executive Officer, of a very large organization. He was most frustrated in his dealings with his senior executives, mostly because he just could not understand why so many of the senior executives who worked for him insisted on constantly telling him what they thought he wanted to hear. This CEO genuinely wanted them to give their own opinions about the issues that were discussed, and he paid them very high salaries to come to grips with problems and recommend solutions. What he got instead was a constant game of his people trying to second guess what he would like them to say and what his own answer would be if he were doing their job.

Lacking the self confidence in their own ability to make decisions and analyze problems, his team members resorted to trying to avoid failure and criticism by setting up a situation where they would at least be perceived as agreeing or being subservient to their boss.

This type of behavior is unfortunately very common and results in a stifling of the career progression of many people and the failure of almost as many organizations. The extent to which it is negative emotionally for the particular person who is in charge, and their compliant managers, differs greatly. However, in almost all the cases I have seen, whether the people stay in the situation or move on, they have a frustrating and unhappy existence.

A key behavior for being successful is to develop the ability to relate confidently to other people on a one to one basis. In doing so, you need to use the very positive views, that you must work to develop, about your own self esteem and self confidence.

Finally, if the boss really does not want to hear what you have to say, you may need to move on anyway, but do give it your best shot as this may still come as a pleasant surprise, particularly if it is a new experience on either side.

Be genuine (Part Two)

There seems to be a continuing disastrous trend based on the philosophy that you can fool some of the people all of the time and all of the people some of the time.

It seems that a firm belief has been developed by many people that as long as you are busy doing either of these two things then you are a smart operator who will survive, and thrive.

There are numerous cases which reinforce this view, but it does not mean that the people who follow these philosophies are personally successful.

I believe it is the general acceptance of the philosophy that all of us get fooled some of the time which allows us to ignore, forgive or just tolerate so many things that we really do not agree with.

This exaggerated example of the 'live and let live philosophy' means that we do not get involved, particularly when it is important that we should, if people make outrageous claims, do outrageous things or do things that harm others.

One should differentiate between people who do their best, fail, admit it and get on with trying again, and those who totally stuff up, make a million excuses and continue stuffing up and blaming their failures on others.

Finally of course there are the straight out swindlers and it is surprising how many of us let them get away with it time and again as well.

The truly successful person will help the hard worker do better, be totally unforgiving of the hopeless excuses given by the non performer and make a formal complaint about the swindler.

Be known as an action person

How often do we hear someone say that a person has initiative or self-motivation? By making yourself known as someone with initiative or as an action person, you will set yourself on a very quick path to success in your chosen field.

It still astounds me that there are so many people who just do not have the attitude or capacity to get on with things.

Many years ago an acquaintance of mine stepped through a glass door in a terrible accident at a party. I had left early so only heard about it later, but apparently everyone there just stood and stared as glass shattered all around him and cut him deeply on the arms, back and legs.

It may have been due to shock (his and theirs), but he was the most composed of all and had to yell 'get organized', and a very brief description of everyone watching him bleed to death, before anyone moved to help.

He was well known as an action man and success came to him for that reason. This small example of how he acted in an emergency is a good illustration of the type of attitude that brings personal success.

I certainly don't suggest putting yourself in dangerous situations to test your capacity to make decision under pressure, although many fast moving sports can certainly help with developing your overall mental as well as physical fitness,

What I do suggest is thinking about how quickly you react on projects that you decide to undertake or how ready you are to present new ideas and help other people. You may find that you do not really rate as well as you would like and might need to give yourself a bit more of a hurry along to succeed.

The Personal Action List (PAL) at the end of this book is a planning guide on how to assess your readiness and how to use your initiative to be more innovative and action oriented. Why not put a few thoughts here on what has occurred to you so far as possible action you might take to be more successful to compare to what you put on the PAL when you finish the book

Be personally resourceful and innovative

It is a fallacy that being innovative or personally resourceful is the province of a very small percentage of the population.

All of us have the capacity to be inventive in so many ways. Once you get it clear in your mind that you can think of better ways of doing things, you open up a whole realm of new possibilities and experiences.

It really is as simple as believing that you can and will think of better ways of doing things.

One of the major drawbacks of most educational systems is that they educate you to rely too much on the information provided. You soon begin to think that everything worthwhile has been thought of, or done, and that being inventive is not part of the equation for you.

If you have now reached your 30th, 40th, 50th year or are past your 70th year for that matter, and have not got that innovative philosophy, do not despair. It really is just a matter of changing your whole way of thinking, but usually starting slowly and allowing your confidence to build.

Depending upon your personality, you may want to work independently, by changing some basic home routines. Alternatively, you may decide to study techniques using any of the numerous books published by authors in the areas of creativity and innovation.

Whatever technique you use, it will almost certainly bring instant results. The real skill is in persisting with your efforts and turning those initial inspiring experiences into longer term changes in your style to make you practically resourceful and innovative in the long term.

Be recognized

One of the key survival strategies for being successful is recognizing the importance of striking a balance between what 'is' and what 'seems to be', between 'achieving' and being 'seen to achieve', between 'perception' and 'reality', between 'presentation' and 'substance'. Much more commonly this is discussed as being aware of the difference between bull dust and brains and having the ability to recognize the importance of each.

These may seem like harsh words, but I recall vividly the example of a very senior and extremely successful person who was concerned, and sought my advice, in relation to the fact that while he had been successful, people that he had worked alongside for years (and he knew to be far less competent than he was) were just as successful.

What is more, he felt that this happened because they were able to present a good image and (as he put it), always fool the people that mattered for just long enough. How could someone so successful devalue his achievements, because he felt others had been successful without having the ability or putting in the hard work..The answer lies in his belief that he could have done more if he had been better at 'promoting' himself,

The key to being truly successful, and contented, is to make sure that you don't become bitter and disillusioned because you do not have the skill to use the right blend of presentation and performance or lack the ability to work with perception as well as reality to achieve your goals.

Stand up and make sure you are recognized for what you do. I am glad to say that this executive and I were able to introduce strategies based on factual performance indicators that brought him the recognition he deserved. You may find it more difficult if you do not have others around you to help you find the way, but if you persist and do your research, you will identify a strategy that works for you. The key is to make sure you have the facts and put the facts forward so that by speaking for themselves, they speak for you as well.

Be trustworthy

One of the most important attributes for achieving personal success is trustworthiness.

Defining trustworthiness, however, is not as easy as it might seem at first glance, but if you think about a person that you know that you really trust, the concept becomes much clearer. Then, when you relate it back to your own image, this personal example gives you something to work towards.

For people to say that someone can be trusted is generally perceived as being a major compliment. To achieve such a compliment requires a significant commitment to respecting the interests of others in every possible way.

Being trustworthy does not just happen, it is a developed characteristic. People who have the capacity to protect the interests of others by not abusing personal information about them, or taking advantage of general personal vulnerability in any way, will have the pleasure of being regarded as trustworthy.

This may seem simple, but it is not. Unfortunately it is very easy to stray from the path of trust.

However, one of the beauties of this particular characteristic is that it is personally rewarding in its own right and those who practice it will need no confirmation of their self worth because they know the value of trust in themselves and others.

An added bonus is that trustworthy people attract other trustworthy people and, conversely, have the ability to recognize people that are not trustworthy.

All in all, there is a terrific multiplier effect that builds both the quality and quantity of trust relationships you develop. The key to getting into the trust business is that you have to be, and stay, trustworthy. It's a life-long process.

Beware the self interest of others

While I always recommend an open and friendly approach to people, it is wise to be on the lookout for that small percentage of the population who put their own interest well in advance of your own and are essentially there to rip you off.

I encountered a person who was having a run of bad luck with some injuries and was looking for some assistance to cope. He showed me an opportunity that existed to get on a mailing list for employment assistance that involved a weekly payment.

Having been a very successful individual with great confidence, up to the time of his rather severe accident, this person was alert to the fact that this probably was not going to be a good investment. However, because his confidence had been affected by his accident, he was wavering.

I was able to confirm his own suspicions that he could make far better use of the money than paying it to a service which was unlikely to ever be of any use to him.

One particular skill in being successful is being aware of the difference between people who have a general skill to provide and those who are preying on the temporary difficulties of others.

A great reward of personal success in this area comes when you become the advisor who keeps other people out of trouble.

We all know the sayings that warn us about things that look too good to be true, being exactly that, but sometimes you need someone to remind you. A key part of being successful is having people you trust on hand to remind you about life's basic rules when you are under pressure and uncertainty creeps in.

Even better, the next time around you will be the adviser and everybody wins.

Celebrate the success of others

It still amazes me how many people do not enjoy seeing the success of others. You should not ever consider that another person's success means that you have failed.

Comparisons are odious and never more so than in assessing your self worth.

Those who are working towards personal success in a constructive way will see the success of others as an opportunity to observe strategies, outcomes and rewards that they can emulate in their approach to their personal challenges.

Feelings of jealousy, envy and so on, only interfere with the constructive process of seeing your world as an essentially non-competitive self-paced opportunity to develop and succeed.

So, if you have negative feelings about the success of others, switch your attention to the work that they have put in to get where they are.

You may be tempted at first to think that no work has been involved, but in my experience success without effort is extremely rare.

Look at the effort others put in, think about your own activities, learn from others who have been there before you, and aim to do as well, or better.

The best solution is to be so absorbed in your own endeavors that there is no time for comparison just the pleasure of comparing successful experiences when you do cooperative work.

The most basic way of looking at this whole situation to make sure you take your work seriously, but do not take yourself that seriously. In other works, if it is all about you and not your work, you have the answer to those feelings of jealousy and envy.

Cherish the family

It is not unusual for me to counsel people who are in difficult circumstances because they have lost their job. It is at these times that I am able to emphasis just how important family is in relation to overall self-esteem, personal security and general success.

One thing that I emphasis most strongly for people with doubt about their own self-worth, is the need to cherish the family.

The family can take on many different connotations for people, but essentially it is about the people who are your personal companions on life's journey. They may live or work with you or may be people you encounter on a day to day basis.

Most simply, family is those people who care where you are, what you are doing and care about what happens to you. These are the people who matter and whose acceptance is critical for your psychological well-being.

It is their support that will see you through the difficult times. Also, by giving them support you build a strong, mutually-fulfilling relationship which is the centre piece of your life.

So if you want to be personally successful, develop a clear perspective of those relationships that form the vocal point of your life, and don't allow yourself to be distracted and distorted by the wider group, who may be in your sphere of influence, but do not have your genuine interests at heart.

Look to your family or other personal confidants to find the opinions and feelings that really matter, but remember it is not a one way street. Also, it is quality that matters. Most of us have just a handful of people in our lives that we completely trust.

The most important thing is to value the relationship.

Choosing a career

Over many years I have counseled numerous people on career choice. One of the things that concerned me most has been the lack of market orientation among the people involved. While factors like interests and capacity are of course most important, the reality about the availability of the jobs, likely salary and career prospects are equally important.

In the success stakes it is very important to have a comprehensive approach to selecting a career. If you know that you want to make a lot of money, then do not set yourself up for a life of frustration by having to swim against the tide in an occupation that is in the lower income earning bracket.

On the other hand, if you know that you will not succeed in something, like sales for example which can be very financially rewarding but is notoriously difficult to do well, do not set yourself up for a life of failure and misery by taking on something that is clearly inappropriate to your interests and your skills.

The key to success is to consider all the factors and to arrive at a balance that will allow you the maximum level of satisfaction, best measured by taking into account all the rewards associated with daily job activity, likely career progress and earning power.

After you have decided what you want to spend the greater part of your life doing, at least for the next few years, you need to makes sure there are jobs available.

Next, you need to map out a plan on how you intend to get the necessary qualifications and skills to do the job. From here on it's about hard work and determination, but if you made the right career choice, the hard work should be fun and the determination should come easy.

Communicate at an appropriate level

Sometimes people have commented on how I change my style of communication, depending on who I am talking to or the group that I am leading.

My view has always been that you should change your style of interacting and presentation to suit the circumstances if you wish to be understood and have your message accepted.

Also, it is common courtesy to avoid embarrassing or alienating your hosts, friends or even complete strangers by responding appropriately to the social requirements of a situation and communicating accordingly.

A very important part of being successful in life is to make people feel comfortable by dressing, speaking and acting in a way that is appropriate to the circumstances.

You do not have to do anything elaborate, although you might choose to, it may be as simple as wearing business clothing when required or being casually dressed when the situation is appropriate.

Similarly, it is a situation of discussing matters that are suitable in the circumstances. It may be most appropriate not to speak about any other than light subjects or, on the other hand, it may be more appropriate to speak about intensive matters such as politics and other social change.

Whatever the situation, it is merely a question of listening and interpreting the demands on the day. This is not difficult but can pay very significant dividends.

Concentrate and focus

Some time ago I had the pleasure to conduct a number of sessions for a group of young sportspeople. It was interesting to see how much personal success strategy training applied to the circumstances of these young people looking to make a career in their chosen sport.

Similarly, their personal characteristics of commitment, concentration and mental focus certainly had a lot to contribute to success in life. Together natural ability, personal characteristics and strategy combined to create champions.

In talking to these athletes about concentration and focus, I highlighted several areas for special attention in the personal focus area.

1) Setting goals and working towards their achievement.
2) A positive and healthy obsession about goals
3) The sense of urgency that has very often been associated with success and is essential as it contributes significantly to concentration and focus in the achievement of short-term goals.
4) Accepting responsibility for your own actions plus an overall sense of social responsibility.
5) Total concentration and focus.

Anyone can use techniques for personal concentration and focus to achieve goals. As I indicated to this group of athletes, it is important to realize that, as with any other skills, these skills must be practiced before there can by any expectation of a positive benefit.

Techniques vary enormously, from the most ancient forms of yoga and Zen practice through to more modern affirmation and visualization techniques, but they all share one characteristic – they are not magic.

As an example, they are tools used by athletes to help bring their natural and trained abilities together to achieve the goal they have aimed for and worked to achieve.

Consider alternatives

There is an old saying that when one door closes another door opens. However, you really have to be very positive about alternatives if something you have been pursuing is suddenly out of your reach and may no longer be attainable.

It is very important if you have been pursuing an attainable goal, or had your heart set on some particular thing, that will just never happen, that you do not allow this to cloud your whole horizon.

If it does, it will stop you considering other opportunities and these new opportunities may, in the final analysis, be just as good as or better than your original goal.

I have spoken over the years to many people where an opportunity to do a course of study, for example, never eventuated, but by bouncing back and considering other options these people ended up having a very successful career.

Others, on the contrary, saw the initial setback as being almost a final statement that they would never achieve their life's goals and dropped their bundle, so to speak, and did not put the same amount of energy into pursuing good alternatives.

Life is just an endless series of pathways and it is a mistake to ever feel that it is just a highway where a road block means that you have literally reached the end of the road. If you want to be successful, you must consider how many options there are and realize that, even though you may focus on one thing for the time being, all of them are available to you, if you need them.

Just as a small exercise, you might like to list some of the things you would do next if for some reason your main career path was suddenly not longer available. You may be surprised by what pleasant alternatives you have or you may find that a little contingency planning is in order.

Consider other peoples' feelings

I have heard it said that to take too much account of other peoples' feelings is a sign of weakness. I believe this is absolutely incorrect and that to have consideration for other people's feelings is a sign of personal strength.

It is also a sign of great personal perception and empathy that leads to the capacity to use knowledge of how other people's emotions work and, thus, help bring about the best possible result for everyone involved in meeting a personal or professional challenge.

Similarly, people often feel that success is all about marching over the top of others and applying the philosophy of the survival of the fittest to every circumstance. Again, this is wrong.

To be successful means to be successful as a human being and a human being is someone who respects the feelings of others no matter who they may be.

So, if you wish to be truly successful, develop skills in understanding how you impact on others and consider the feelings of others in what you do.

In most cases there will be an immediate reward in seeing personal development in others that will be sufficient for you to know that you have managed the circumstances in a professional and caring way.

More importantly you will feel personally rewarded at the development and application of a vital people skill. The best part of this is that it gets better with time and practice.

Over time, this approach develops into a long standing personal philosophy that makes everything you do a contribution to making enhancing peoples' lives and making the world a better place.

Controlling aggression

We all get frustrated at different times because situations do not go the way we would like or because we are not being able to control a situation or another person as we think we should be able to.

Often, this can happen in situations with children who very often do not respond the way adults, particularly those with little experience, would like them to.

Very often the outcome of this frustration is a feeling of aggression generated by the idea that the other person is being aggressive towards you.

One of the keys to being successful in life is to be able to defuse this aggression and replace it with appropriate assertive behavior or, if all else fails, to get out of the situation for a time and return to it only when you are able to deal with it in a constructive manner.

The best technique for defusing or transforming this aggression is to form a picture clearly in your mind that the aggression is not focused on you.
Usually, it is being projected from the other person in a random way and you just happen to be in the surrounding area.

In this way, whether you have particular responsibility for the other person or are just an unrelated bystander, you can formulate a strategy based on a planned intervention rather than an emotional defense of your own ego.

Remember, if all else fails, provided you do not leave the other person open to an even worse outcome than if you stayed around, just get out of the situation and come back later.

The time out from the situation also, lets you think about the situation before doing anything. This is particularly useful if some action is expected by you, because doing it in the heat of the moment is, usually, not a good idea.

Control, do not be controlled

One of the biggest mistakes people make in their personal organizing is being put off their plan, because they are overpowered by other people's priorities. Amazingly, these priority busters are often not aware of the impact they are making on your progress.

Without being exploitive of other people, it is very important to set your focus in relation to what you want to achieve and to make sure you do not become a puppet or a bouncing ball who responds just too readily to the demands of other people. You need to accept only what works for you.

A great way to get underway with this strategy is to use the eighty-twenty rule that says that 20% of what you do is going to account for 80% of the results you get.

At first you are going to need to think very carefully and spend what seems an inordinate amount of time deciding whether what you are about to do is part of the twenty percent that gives you 80% of the effect or part of the 80% that gives you only 20% of the effect.

It is worth taking the time to sort this out as it becomes you agenda for achievement and success.

Fortunately the beauty of this process is that it is a very easy concept to grasp and, when applied repeatedly, can bring about an overall improvement in the use of your time and personal resources.

It may be something of a slow painful beginning but it is well worthwhile suffering the pain to establish a permanent focus on being in control of those factors which contribute most to your success.

So, get into the habit of closely scanning other peoples' demands and checking them against your agenda. If they are part of the 20% that get 80% of your result, add them to your agenda and you will find you stay in control.

Count your blessings

I was driving along the road the other day when I saw a group of care givers wheeling a number of special needs children on an outing.

This really brought home to me once again the wisdom of counting your blessings in achieving personal success in life, but also the reinforced my long held view that everybody can and should be able reach their potential.

My father repeated often one of his favorite sayings about the philosopher who said 'I thought I was badly off because I had no shoes until I saw a man with no feet'. Life is a continuum and there will always be people who are better off than you are and people who are worse off than you are. Depending on your situation, you can play your part by giving where you can.

The clue to being personally successful is positioning yourself with a positive frame of mind in relation to your lot in life. Often it is amazing how those with, apparently, the least to be happy about are not only content with their approach to what they have, but want to give to those still less fortunate.

There is no end to the magic of the human spirit. This does not mean that you base your own happiness on the unhappiness of others, but it does mean that life at all levels provides all of us with opportunities to be successful each in our own way.

Making that philosophy work is all about counting your blessings in the hand that has been dealt to you in life's great card game and playing that hand in the most positive and capable way that you can.

Seeing these people working together to get the most out of life made me all that more aware that mental attitude is a big percentage of personal success, on the part of all us if, no matte if we are giving or receiving.

Decide for yourself

Do not let other people decide what you are going to do.

A big part of being successful is being able to decide to continue a job or activity that you do well, and enjoy, and ensure that you are recognized for the contribution that you make.

Standing by your beliefs and being respected for being honest with yourself and others, is vital when discussing your life goals.

For example, one of my consulting staff was required to recruit a new person for a job and, despite writing a quite restrictive and demanding advertisement, received in excess of 100 applications. He seemed concerned and I queried the reason.

He said that in speaking to the candidates, he found that many of them were in good positions already and were unable to say why they were seeking a change, other than for the money or just for the sake of a change.

This lack of a comprehensive change strategy was quite foreign to my successful team member, because he had always based any move on a thorough analysis of dissatisfaction with one job or extreme attraction to another.

The message for all of us is to not be driven to change by other people in the form of peer group pressure. Assess your situation and decide what you want to do.

If you are happy, do not let other people unsettle you. The grass is definitely not always greener on the other side of the fence.

Also, loyalty does not mean blind loyalty. If you are happy and doing well, you need to give credit to the people that are making this happen. Hopefully you will be in their position one day and the loyalty will then be transferred to you.

Define those top qualities

One thing we should all do in our quest for personal success is make sure that we are very clear about the personal attributes we have for making life a success.

Doing a mini audit on your skills, and comparing your skills to the challenges that you are undertaking, lets you get a much clearer picture of the strategies you should implement to capitalize on your opportunities.

In business, a SWOT analysis means looking at strengths, weaknesses, opportunities and threats. This is just as important in personal success. It is a very simple process.

You just list your strengths, your weaknesses, what opportunities are available to you in the world at large and what are the threats to your achieving overall personal success.

You can then list your objectives, where you want to go, and your strategies, how you want to get there, in full awareness of the tools you have available to you.

I recommend this SWOTOS (Strengths, Weaknesses, Opportunities, Threats, Objectives, and Strategies) approach to corporations and individuals on a regular basis.

Not only is it important to do for a first time, but you have to use it and keep it up to date.

I am often asked to list the biggest threats to making a strategic plan successful. I have done elaborate versions of this process with corporations, but the answer is no different for individuals. You have to have the skills, the resources and the motivation to make even the best plan work.

Develop people skills

I spoke recently with an executive who I knew to be highly intelligent and skillful and who, in many ways, would have been regarded as very successful. However, he found that his further development was blocked by his inability to work well with people in difficult situations.

This reinforced for me just how much interpersonal or people skills are vital for success in every situation. Even if they are not the central theme of your activities, such as with highly technical positions that require little interaction, interpersonal skills still are required professionally and socially, particularly if you want to take on a senior leadership role.

With relationships, like any skill, if you just step out and try some particular social technique 'live' for the first time it will normally not go well.

Practice makes perfect with interpersonal skills as it does with any sporting activity.

You have to be prepared to invest time in planning a strategy about what you are going to say and rehearsing the lines in your mind.

So, if you have problems in this important area, take the initiative and complete one of the many communications courses available.

One long standing, but still very valid, approach is to do a public speaking course and/or join one of the many public speaking clubs in your area. After you have completed the course or joined the club, it is just a matter of practice, practice, practice.

You will find that even the most basic improvement in how you deal with people on a day to day basis will make you feel much happier. Also, one success will lead to another in your quest for better interpersonal skills.

Develop your own reward system

It is interesting with all the talk about macro economics and micro economics that so little attention is paid to individual economics.

We all have our little economic system revolving around our day to day activities and a better understanding of it can help us greatly in motivating ourselves to achieve our goals.

The beauty of this individual economy is that it is controlled by you, you are the treasurer, the secretary and the president or whatever title you want to give yourself and you can choose to impose taxes, give windfall gains, or administer any plus or minus you choose.

Too often we all look outside our own individual economy and think all those micro economic pressures in day to day bill paying and wage earning, and the macro economic pressures from world events have us totally at their mercy.

The fact is, in pure enjoyment terms, they are pretty far removed from the personal enjoyment decisions you can make about things as basic, but highly pleasurable, as going to sit outside in the sun for half an hour.

So if you have a fixation about events that are outside you, and probably beyond your control, try focusing in, it will not take you long to work out just how many things there are that you can control.

The crazy thing is, they are all happening regularly on a day to day basis and you are letting all the fun of controlling them slip right through your fingers.

Living for today is not escapism; it is an essential part of enjoying life.

Develop your own style

One thing that many people seem to forget is our uniqueness as human beings.

I am still amazed by how many people still describe things as quite unique or very unique when the whole point of being unique is being the only one of a type.

There is no quite or very when you are one of a kind. You must remember that you are the only one of your type.

You are as unique as your fingerprint.

The great thing is that this uniqueness extends well beyond your fingerprints and really should be a central part of the enjoyment of your life.

In fact, I believe that a key part of personal success is realizing that this uniqueness exists and developing it.

I am not suggesting a crazy egomaniacal shrine in your bedroom, but I do recommend a keen appreciation of the truth that you as a person are different from everyone else and have a unique contribution to make to the world.
To be personally successful, you have to have a firm belief in your uniqueness to help you establish your identity in a world that often seems crowded and can make you doubt your own significance and worth. So think about it.

You are the only you. Realizing this, enjoying it and living with this thought clearly in your mind is an important part of personal success.

Developing good habits

I spoke to a person who was concerned that developing good habits meant losing control of your life and living like a robot.

This is certainly not the case. If you have worked out a situation where being in a routine helps you achieve goals, ones that you have decided are important to you, then habits are terrific tools for being successful.

In fact, in changing behaviors that you are not happy with, developing a routine that substitutes a new behavior for the old behavior is highly desirable.

If you find you cannot control your weight for example because every night you sit down in front of the television set with a big helping of some dessert, try this,

Develop a routine where you serve, wrap up and freeze seven small desserts for the week, preferably after you have just eaten a huge dessert and do not feel particularly hungry, can be very productive.

The thing about good habits is that they require planning and effort, while bad habits require no planning and no effort. However, when planned and implemented, good habits become as easy as bad habits and no longer require planning because they are a, you guessed it – a habit.

Habits do not have to be bad habits and, like the case of the champion sportsman who could never remember a single day when he did not exercise, they can be good habits even when they are obsessive and completely bound up with your whole way of life.

So, just sort out the habits that work for you and build them into your routine. They are part of you successfully managing your life. Getting rid of the bad habits will be harder. However, if you have developed good habits, then substituting new good habits for old bad ones should be easier.

Developing good study habits

Invariably when you speak to people about study and success, they have a lot of problems, particularly with procrastination.

One of the small techniques that I have found particularly helpful in overcoming study procrastination problem is launching into the project as soon as possible.

One of the reasons that people have problems with study, and tend to procrastinate, is their major fear that they will not be able to cope with the challenge.

When you launch yourself into it immediately, you get close to the problem and discover that it is not as daunting as you thought.

If you avoid the study situation, your fear level is maintained and, eventually, when you are forced to get into the situation by the approaching deadline, you still discover it is not so daunting after all.

However, by that time you have inevitably left yourself too little time to use your new found knowledge about your ability to cope.

So if you want to beat that study habit problem, launch into the work as soon as the work is given to you. When you know what you are up against, you will not find it anywhere near as difficult as you imagined it to be and you will have the time to do a really good job.

One last point, this is a major issue because it is not as easy as it sounds. Do not program a marathon session to get under way.

Just allocate a small amount of time, about 30 minutes, but have the material you need to understand fully what has to be done. That way you will not get overwhelmed and bogged down on your first attempt. Continue if you want to, but be ready to take a break and come back and start again when you are fresh.

Do not accept false idols

In considering the issue of images that should be rejected because they provide poor brain food, I was disappointed to speak to a young woman who had rejected a business career because of her knowledge of successful business people and associated negative feelings about how they achieved their success.

This woman still entered into a very worthwhile career, but I could not help but feel that her inability to reject these false idols may have contributed to her rejecting a more challenging career which may have resulted in her contributing more significantly to the community.

It is very hard when working in a subordinate position in any organization to see past the false idols that are paraded before you and avoid the negative images of leaders in general.

However, it is extremely important to understand that the rejection of these negative images and the control of your own input is an important part of the happiness in, happiness out formula.

Parents need to work with their children on the happiness in, happiness out formula to make sure that they can recognize these false idols and not let them contribute towards knee jerk reactions in relation to their own future.

Using happiness in, happiness out should help in blotting out negative people and their influence on the thoughts, activities and ambitions of a young person.

The beauty of being young or new to the happiness in, happiness out formula is that the impact is just that much more dramatic and more enjoyable.

There will be negatives enough in life, without adding lack of recognition of the importance of choice in interpreting life's events.

Do not accept hypocrisy

It's a sad situation that there is so much hypocritical behavior in society. People who are on the road to success will certainly not accept this behavior as normal and will strive to work with people who are determined, able to practice what they preach and give credit where credit is due.

Unfortunately, the development of a facade and the reaping of rewards in total disproportion to effort expended has become something of a well developed frame of reference and strategy for many people. However, genuine success still comes from pursuing goals that are worthwhile on a level playing field.

It may seem old fashioned but I believe the promotion of a reward system based on equity rather than the ability to generate success by playing the system should still be a key part of true success.

In the longer term, this the success of this philosophy rests with people who strive for success by making long ranging personal and ethical decisions driven by their conscience. Regrettably, differing definitions of conscience can make this an area of conjecture in its own right.

As definitions conscience vary so much, it is important to have an inner commitment that means your short, medium and long range goals and achievements and commitment that is consistent with your values and your actions.

In this way , if you are honest with yourself you will always be able to assess the merit or otherwise of your achievements, and the strategies you used to get there, and avoid the trap of hypocrisy that so many people fall into.

And what is the point? Only you can truly determine that.

Do not be angry about the weaknesses of others

In building your own happiness model, one of the most difficult things to do is to remain positive about the weaknesses of others. All people have shortcomings and the closer we are to people, the more aware we will be of those shortcomings.

It is very easy to think of building your own happiness model by being angry and rejecting the perceived negative aspects of those close to us, negativity which we think results from their weaknesses.

Parents particularly come in for quite a deal of negativity from their children because of parental weaknesses to which their children are exposed.

A positive approach to dealing with the possible negativity arising out of the weaknesses of one's parents, other family members or friends is to recognize only the true happiness components as providing any useful input to your own happiness.

Rather than fighting what you perceive to be the negative aspects, work with the happiness behaviors and let the negative emotions slide right on by.

Clearly, this is not an easy task but even as an exercise in clearly recognizing behaviors and emotions that contribute to your happiness and those that do not, it is worth doing.

Any contribution that this recognition of positive behaviors makes to you not becoming angry in a relationship is a bonus.

Relationship dynamics is always a challenge and applying the happiness in/happiness out philosophy that rejects counter-productive emotional negatives is a good strategy for maintaining the overall positive feeling in a relationship.

Do not brow beat people

In listening to the newly appointed Chief Executive of a business organization introduce himself at a meeting, I was astounded at how this senior person had no concept of how to present himself subtly to the audience.

In circumstances which required subtlety and feeling, but forthrightness, he got the whole thing back to front. His delivery was extremely forthright, had absolutely no finesse and took no account of the audience's feelings.

Around me I could feel people wishing him off the stage and cringing at some of the presentation. Clearly, this person had not done his research and completely alienated the audience as a result.

If you have to make a presentation, make sure you understand your role in the situation and prepare accordingly. Be aware of the audience's needs and feelings and make the presentation appropriate to meet those needs.

Nobody likes to be thumped into submission, even when the circumstances give the presenter the opportunity to use that technique. Moreover, if the best technique is one of subtlety and a bashing is given, the situation deteriorates into being laughable.

This strategy applies to individual interactions as well as speaking to groups. How many times have you heard the comment made that a person only listens to what the other person is saying so they can catch their breath and continue making their point.

Simply put, know your audience. Consider their needs, not just your own. Avoid, at all costs, brow beating the audience instead of communicating.

If you do this, you can pick the communication style to suit the occasion and you, and your audience, will be a winner every time.

Do not ignore the silent types

In doing a major survey of employees in an organization recently, I had the great pleasure to meet the classic quiet achiever.

This lady had worked for the organization for some years and had risen to a position of quite some responsibility. The significant thing about this particular person was her apparent lack of ambition. She certainly had not aspired to be in charge of her work area and had no aspirations for further promotion.

Interestingly, she had been given a share of this quite substantial business without even indicating any interest in being rewarded in that way.

It is important to realize that these quite achievers do exist. It is a great regret to me that I often find them in organizations, but being totally ignored and undervalued.

The tragedy for their employers is that, if they are undervalued, the quiet achievers do not wait around working for people who do not merit their respect. Many organizations lose these valuable people without even realizing that they have existed.

Successful people are aware of the existence of these quiet achievers, work closely with them and share their success. Furthermore, successful managers are those that go out of their way to find and reward these people.

So if you encounter quieter people, do not assume that quietness relates to lack of ability or enthusiasm. Quite the opposite can be true.

Truly successful people see value in all people, well beyond their superficial characteristics, and go out of their way to make sure that both parties get rewarded, both financially and philosophically by through working on a basis of mutual respect.

Do not invite danger

One of the strangest things about the uncontrolled, unpredictable garbage in, garbage out management of our own brains is the fact that we so often invite other people to fill our heads with rubbish. There seems to develop early in everyone's life a view that intuition, independent thinking and personal confidence should run a long second to being taught routine things, working to team rules and following the tried and true path.

Yes, rules have a very important purpose and we would be a very poor society without them, but they can become a law without reason and stifle creativity and progress. That is the danger I am warning you about. So often I have found in doing assessments that people, who are really successful, particularly in establishing new ventures, are those who have a very high score on a measure of independent thinking. These people do not need the approval of others for their entrepreneurial ideas.

They do not necessarily reject other peoples' ideas; indeed they usually get the best professional advice. They just do not feel a need to go to other people and obtain their approval purely to reinforce that what they are doing is worthwhile and will be successful, either personally or in business.

So once again, the Happiness In, Happiness Out philosophy is a winner for those people who are independent thinkers because they have a personality trait which says to them they don't need the opinion of others emotionally, because their own thoughts are entirely adequate for their needs.

However, a word of warning is important. Positive thoughts are never a substitute for good research, the best available techniques, and the highest quality in implementation. The whole concept of positive thinking is about building a confident approach to counteracting baseless negativity. It is not about ignoring quality advice. So, basic business and success rules are there for a good purpose, but you should not let them stifle your creativity.

Do not just take or just give

We are all familiar with the expression - give and take. Certainly in relationships in everyday life and in the work situation, give and take has a central part to play.

When it works successfully, it is a key part of any successful relationship. If does not work, it can be harmful in both the short and long term. The key to success is to get the balance right.

Those who aspire to be successful realize that to give in any of these relationships is absolutely essential. On the other hand, they would also be aware that being alert for the other person taking rather than receiving is important.

It is a fine line, but the difference between people receiving what you give or taking from you, willing or otherwise, can be the beginning of the end for many relationships, business or personal. To be successful it is essential to make it clear that, while you give and are happy to see people receive, being 'taken' is not on your agenda.

In addition, it is advisable to get in early if you think a relationship is heading down this track. The more committed you are the harder it gets to make adjustments or get out.

When people realize that you are not going to be a doormat, they will either respect you more and stop taking from you or they will go elsewhere so they can find a doormat that they can walkover and continue their selfish behavior.

If you want to be successful you will be one of the people who sets the guidelines very clearly and very early that, while you give and like to see people receive, you will not be taken advantage of. Be aware, it can be very difficult to manage these situations, which is why business and personal counselors exist. Do not hesitate to get professional assistance if you need it.

Do not let others get you down

One of the areas to which I have devoted most of my time in career development is helping people to reach their optimum level of chosen performance. Unfortunately, helping others succeed can be difficult when you are up against spoiling tactics from 'put down' people, who should really be helping, but seem to believe that keeping others subservient is important for maintaining their own position of strength and authority.

Furthermore, my long term finding is that these put down people just do not change. They keep putting people down, usually to battle their own insecurity. For this reason, the only solution is to get out from under quickly and move to a situation where you are able to control your own destiny. If you do have to work for someone else, choose someone who will support you and open the way for you to succeed, on a basis of mutual respect and mutual achievement.

One of the worst things about these put down situations is trying to see beyond being stuck under the influence of someone who is so negative. Many of these put down people are particularly skilful at eroding peoples' confidence, and making them think that there is no way out. Of course this is total rubbish and very often the people being victimized are doing very successful things in other areas, such as sport or hobbies, and will succeed in a new supportive job environment.

There are a few simple tests that you can use about your relationships with people in senior positions. Just ask the following questions. Are you praised or abused?' 'Are you kept informed or kept in the dark?' 'Do you speak positively or negatively about the person you work for'

If you answered negatively to any of these questions you need to think very seriously about getting out and finding yourself a new positive working life. There are good people out there, but the onus is on you to go out and find them in order to achieve personal success.

Do not sell yourself short

So often we just do not give ourselves sufficient credit for the quality of our own skills and the achievements that we have behind us.

It is important to realize your self-worth without becoming full of your own self-importance, so that you can represent yourself properly in any situation.

Many times, I have had to counsel people who have been exploited in the workplace. This exploitation often came about because of the individual's poor economic circumstances and the pressure this put on them.

Particularly when you seem under pressure and there is no one around who can help you, it is important to give yourself credit for the skills that you have and to make sure that you are not exploited.

There are of course government agencies that can help you but so often the situations are marginal and it is your own self-esteem and self-confidence that is needed to win the day.

This is where family and friends, who are positive about your skills, can help as well. So do not underrate yourself and do not let other people underrate you.

The other avenue that people tend to overlook is the world of the private recruitment agent. There are many agencies, and some are very specialized. They should have a very strong knowledge of the market to do their job and can give you advice as part of the job search process. Also, they should operate completely confidentially.

So, if you feel you are selling yourself short, there are many avenues available to get advice, or another job. You just have to make the first move.

Effort versus results

Over the years, I have had numerous opportunities to assess people accurately by virtue of the results that they achieve in psychological assessments. This has really confirmed in my mind the belief that the appearance of activity or success can be totally unrelated to actual results. It is most important to work to full capacity when you are working.

One employee, who I recall vividly, worked virtually the minimum prescribed hours. However, when he was at work, he did nothing but work and he worked to 100% of his capacity.

Strangely, the ability to work to 100% capacity is very rare. Needless to say, the individual that works in this way achieves the same outstanding results as my very memorable employee.

The key factor in being successful is to determine very clearly what brings results and work with that formula to make the best use of your time.

It is a fact that we all fall into habit patterns, whether they are good or bad. Developing good habit patterns is just a matter of hard work, setting small and then larger goals for change, and sticking to what we resolve.

Of course, there are numerous distractions for any course of change but in this area, being successful always comes back to you, your motivation, your resolve and getting the best outcome in the area of effort versus results.

Successful people take responsibility for their own lives, work out the success formula for them and apply it. Strange as it might seem the key is to think big, but start small.

Get the formula right on some simple tasks and build from there. The stronger the foundation, the better it supports the bigger and more complex challenges you will face on your journey of success.

Emotions and business

Reading recently of a sensational business failure, reminded me of one of the most basic elements for personal success.

Do not get emotionally dependent on your product or service to the point where you lose sight of why you are in business.

In this particular case, the individual was running the business to satisfy his own needs instead of the needs of the potentially hundreds of thousands of customers that he wanted. The end result was that he didn't win over the various customers but continued to produce his product at great cost until he lost everything.

While enthusiasm for your product or service is absolutely essential, it should never be at the expense of market awareness. If you are your own major customer that will be all well and good but that is not how life works.

If you want to be successful, balance your enthusiasm for how good your product or service by being aware of the cold hearted reality that if other people do not think you have a great product, you are headed for business failure.

Business, like life, is about understanding peoples' wants and needs and the fact that they are not always the same as your own. Understand them well and you will do well, ignore them and you are more than likely doomed to failure.

So, while real passion for what you do and the products or services that you produce is critical, realism about your market will always have the last say. If you find you are not making the sales and revenue you want you may need to direct your passion elsewhere.

The beauty of self employment is that you can choose what you want to do. Just do it before circumstances mean you have no choice.

Empathy

Empathy is the ability to appreciate another person's feelings without yourself becoming so emotionally involved that your judgment is affected. It sharpens our perception in all sorts of situations in our daily lives and work. It helps us to increase our understanding and enjoyment of other people. It is a state of mind which anyone can develop and improve.

We can acquire empathy through role-playing, either in a real situation or by virtual role playing as I will explain. One of the biggest mistakes we make in dealing with others is to underestimate the importance of their feelings. To grasp the essential feeling-pattern of another person, try to put yourself in their shoes. The first step is to truly understand what they are like. You cannot assume that others feel exactly as you do when faced with a situation. Empathy requires you to forget your own reactions and attempt to see the world through the eyes of the other person.

All of us practice empathy at times without knowing it. Developing meaningful relationships with others would be difficult without it. The trick is to learn to apply this approach consciously and deliberately. There is little we cannot learn about others if we can tune in to the feelings and thoughts behind their words and actions.

Of course the ideal process is one where the other person is an active participant and is learning just as much about you as you are about them. In addition to improving social interpersonal interaction, an awareness of how others think and feel can be the key to effective leadership and management.

In this situation, the process is normally going to be two way because your team members will usually analyse your leadership style, consciously or unconsciously. So, be it work or personal, put yourself in the other person's position. You will find it a good starting point for developing empathy.

Entrepreneurial success

A 20 year old student was discussing with me her dreams for being a business success. Although she had thought of numerous ventures that she might take on, none of them had inspired her to go ahead, particularly after investigating the detail of what was required.

I explained that one of the key elements in being successful in an entrepreneurial situation was to identify a challenge that she would enjoy minute by minute, hour by hour, day by day for as long as she was involved.

Because none of the options that she had considered up to that time had this ongoing built in reward system, she had not felt sufficiently inspired to follow through.

What she was looking for, I said, was a project that would get her excited and keep her excited throughout its lifetime. So, if you are contemplating entrepreneurial activities, keep in mind the need to feel inspired or excited about your project. Being self employed and pursuing your own destiny should most definitely be fun as well as highly profitable.

The search for projects of this type is not usually easy. Success is obtained as much by knowing which opportunities to reject as which to pursue. In this regard, you will hear it said that many business people failed many times before they finally succeeded. This is true, but it is not compulsory.

It is far better to learn from the mistakes of others. Even though it may not have the same impact, it is a lot less painful. It is far better to sort out the potential failures by good research.

So remember, don't be disappointed at discovering that a great opportunity is not so great. The weeding out process is the key to finding the project that will succeed.

Environmental awareness

On a training program I conducted, I noticed that while we were doing outside exercises one of the participants just left rubbish where it fell or threw it vaguely in the direction of where someone else might pick it up.

In these days when burn bash and bury has well and truly been superseded by 'if you must create rubbish take it with you and dispose of it properly', I immediately wondered if this total disregard for society's current trends might be reflected in this persons personality.

In this case, this particular individual turned out to be inconsiderate of his colleagues in a number of other significant ways. More importantly, he was not able to acknowledge, to them or to himself, that he was at fault.

It was also extremely interesting that efforts by other people on the program to influence this person were limited because of his particularly strong attitudes. Other members of his team felt it was not their place to criticize him while they had weaknesses themselves, even though the team suffered as a result of this failure to take action on one team member's major destructive weaknesses.

This incident reminded me that truly successful people do not allow fear about their own weaknesses to draw them away from the pursuit of what is a worthwhile belief, even if it means criticizing the weaknesses of others.

It is true that people in glasses houses should not throw stones, but if we do nothing about major things because we have minor faults, there will be no end to the spiral of negativity.

So, if you encounter blatant negativity, be it environmental or otherwise, do not hesitate to speak up in defense of the group, society or the planet.

Every dog does not have its day

There is a very popular saying that every dog has its day. It is a saying popularized by people who believe that chance and fate should play a bigger part in their success or failure than their own efforts.

People do not all get their just desserts, every dog does not have its day. Some people just continue to win while others lose and, of course, life is not fair in many ways. If it was fair, it wouldn't be life it would be robot world. If you want to be successful then do <u>not</u> develop the habit of shrugging your shoulders and saying that a failure will be sorted out in the swings and roundabouts.

A failure is exactly that - a failure. I am not suggesting that you need to beat yourself about the head every time you fail to achieve your goals. Just do not rationalize everything by saying it will work out better next time, because that would be a fair outcome.

Have you ever noticed how some people seem to bob up in the headlines all the time? Some people seem to win all the time. That is not an accident. Those people put in the effort and work very hard to succeed.

So if you want to be successful; get stuck into it, make every goal post a winner. Winning and losing can both become habits and the key to success is choosing to win. The essential lesson is that success is not about luck. It is about hard work and learning what works best so that your hard work is not wasted.

By the way, that is not to say that you should not have a sense of humour and invest in having some fun where luck is supposed to be the key to success, lottery tickets and so on, just keep your main investment where your skills determine the outcome.

Extended family

One of the things I have noticed about successful people is that they appear to build their friendship network like an extended family. That is, their friends become very close and are openly advised of activities, goals and secrets on a basis that is normally reserved for the immediate family.

This extended family is not necessarily a very large group of people, but certainly those that are allowed into this inner sanctum are very close.

This philosophy seems to be unconscious, but still seems to build a tight knit group which gives tremendous support for the individual. It is amazing how this binding of friends can make the standard activities of the individual concerned that much larger than life. It brings the individual into a team environment on an ongoing basis and they seem to be never without support.

This networking all seems to arise from characteristics of trust and enthusiasm that the truly successful person brings to their relationships. It is certainly not an unlimited trust, but where there is clear evidence that trust is warranted it is given and most often returned.

You might like to analyze your own relationships and, if you find that a high level of trust is part of your scenario, perhaps an experiment with a very close friend might give you a chance to look at some new opportunities to develop your personal 'team'.

However, a word of warning is in order. I have seen people try to do this in an artificial and manipulative way and it was a disaster. The worst part was that these people were generally oblivious to the negative impact they were making.

If this does not come naturally to you, leave it for others and develop your own networking approach. As long as you are genuine and there is something in it for all concerned, you will be on safe ground.

Feed yourself positive feelings

It is fascinating to see that while so much attention is paid to the improvement of diet in the modern world, that there is little comparable work done on feeding yourself positive thoughts.

It seems to me that if you are what you eat in body terms then in mental terms you have to be what you see, hear, smell and touch.

With your sense of hearing accounting for the bulk of your emotional sensory input, it would seem to make a lot of sense to control as much as possible the positivity of what you hear.

This is really quite simple, when you think about it, because you spend all of your time in your own company and probably spend more time talking to yourself than anyone else. In other words you have almost total control over your own thoughts and the associated input unless you choose to abandon control to other forces.

No matter how it is presented, this self-talk concept makes sense. In fact, it is a very deep philosophical concept that has been pondered through the ages on the basis of our need to know if there is more to us than flesh and blood. This spiritual discussion is fascinating, but the trick for achieving your success is to keep it simple and just use positive self-talk on the basis that the more positive thoughts you squeeze in the more positive you will feel and the more positive output you will achieve.

The key issue to consider is the way this self talk builds your resilience and level of positivity. In this way you are more resistant to negative influences and more able to take a positive approach to your daily challenges. The desire to feel good and be positive is one reason why motivational speakers are so popular. Another reason is because the positive input has a limited life and you have to go back regularly. This is why the effects are more long lasting if you can do it yourself.

Feet of clay stay that way

It has always surprised me how many people are overwhelmed, intimidated, daunted or in awe of academic or other qualifications. Respect and reward for ability is certainly very positive and we should do everything that we can to promote achievement in ourselves and in others. However, having unrealistic expectations or perceptions of other individuals, especially because of the position they hold or the qualifications they have gained, can be quite dangerous.

All that obtaining a qualification proves is that the person is able to obtain qualifications, pass exams or whatever. Any further conclusions that one draws about people must be balanced by a close examination of what skill they have demonstrated beyond the most basic qualification.

As much as some people might like to convince us otherwise, all people are different. They will always have different levels of skill. The differences may be minute on occasions (mostly they are not), but they will still vary. So while the title may say soldier, sailor or candlestick maker, do not expect to get the same defense, safe passage or quality of trade work from different people with the same title.

There is some comfort in knowing that the longer the period of training, such as in medicine, the more likely it will be that you receive consistency in quality of service. In addition, the existence of regulatory boards and professional associations adds to the enforcement of this quality.

Nevertheless, successful people choose their service providers based on knowledge of their ability, not a piece of paper. No matter what type of provider you are looking for, get information on that person's achievements to date, preferably from other customers. The more important the job, the more important it is to get a number of references.

Fight for your rights

It was emphasized to me so clearly once again recently, in counseling someone who had been poorly treated by their employer, that there comes a time that you must stand up and fight for your rights.

It is all very well to go through life with a conciliatory and co-operative attitude, but one should never allow one's dignity, and the welfare of one's family, to be mercilessly trodden on.

In this case an employer had acted totally ruthlessly and inhumanely and attempted to smooth over the situation by virtually brainwashing the person involved.

It is very important in being personally successful to be aware that there are certain situations, hopefully not happening too often, where you do have to fight.

Also when you do fight, do it with all your might and with all your personal skill and support systems. Keeping in mind, I am talking about a legal battle here, not a physical one.

It is rare for me to speak about total assertiveness, but it is a personal success strategy that must be kept in the bag of tricks for when it is necessary to battle with an aggressor who has no morals and can be dealt with in no other way.

A word of warning, do not let your standards slip by getting too close to you enemy and acquiring some of the standards of your opponent. Think and act smart, but leave the dirty pool to the other side otherwise the path to personal success will become awfully slippery and unrewarding.

Focus

One of the key characteristics for being successful is the capacity to focus very clearly on your target.

It is almost as though you must draw mentally two big black lines down the edges of your vision to keep distractions away from your image of what you wish to achieve.

Certainly, people that are very successful not only have obsessive thoughts about their goal but also the ability to block out thoughts that intrude on their progress towards achieving what they want.

It is a situation very similar to meditation where you have to focus on smaller and smaller images to build your mental concentration. Focus in goal achievement is very much the same.

The more clearly that you can build a picture of the goal you are seeking, the more likely it is that you will be able to persevere with activities that are directed towards that goal.

So if you have a goal in mind, do not be concerned if you dream about it, think about all day and just cannot get it out of your mind. This is a very positive indication that you are focused on it very clearly and will work very constructively towards its achievement.

Just do not be fooled into thinking that thinking is enough. Just as the sales executive says that 'nothing happens until somebody sells something', the achiever knows that nothing happens until you make the dream a reality by your actions.

You cannot will a goal into achievement, your focus is just a tool to support your ability to construct and implement a really good plan.

Forget swings and roundabouts

A lot of people, who are unjustly dealt with by someone, comfort themselves by thinking that the person will have their day in court, so to speak. My finding is that, not only is this not the case very often, but to live with this belief, particularly to somehow rationalize a bad experience, is very negative.

Having a firm grasp of the realities of life, and maintaining an associated personal philosophy based on dealing with things positively and in a controlled way, is much more appropriate for achieving personal success than believing that the bad people of the world will get their due.

It is much more appropriate to work on the principle that you will be recognized for your own achievements rather than leaving it to some mysterious process of natural justice to even out the experiences of life.

People who are going to be personally successful will attribute success or otherwise to their own activities and will lay any blame for failure firmly at their own door.

A very old adage says that it is wise to change the things that you are capable of changing, sensible to accept those things that you cannot change and important to know which is which. It is certainly much more productive to focus your efforts on the areas where you can take control and make the necessary changes and not waste your resources on unwinnable battles.

As a much more modern sage has told me so many times, there is the easy way and the hard way, the smart way and the dumb way, strangely the easy smart way is often available (and completely moral as well as legal). However, even the easy smart way is still a lot of work.

Fulfill your obligations

It is amazing just how much of a negative impact one small incident of unreliability can have on your profile.

One important aspect of being personally successful is to develop a reputation for fulfilling your obligations.

If people are relying on you, do not let them down. Make sure that you do not make commitments that you are not going to meet.

It is far better to say no and not get involved than to over commit yourself and find that you are constantly letting people down.

Your reputation will soon suffer and quite correctly because you have embarrassed people and caused them inconvenience purely through your own lack of consideration.

So think about how much time you have available and what your capabilities are and only commit yourself to obligations that you know you can fulfill.

Conversely, keep a balance and do not let yourself become a slave to others by volunteering to do everything for everyone. You will just as quickly fall by the wayside if you try to do the impossible.

So do what you can, do it well, and all will be well, because you will have a reputation for being reliable and delivering on your promises.

Most importantly, this will become a habit that helps you deliver on promises to yourself as well as others and, when you think about, not letting yourself down is a key part of making sure you have the ability to not disappoint others.

Get in touch with your feelings

It strikes me that many people have a problem with acknowledging their inner- most feelings. Experiencing feelings of fear (even dread), turmoil, jealousy, passion, boredom and so on is a basic part of life.

Too often people have been told that they should deny the existence of these innermost feelings, because being stable, disciplined and well organized is being normal.

Certainly, reacting anti-socially to any of these intense feelings is something that our society has decided is not acceptable, but this does not mean that we should deny that these feelings exist.

On the contrary, suppressing them can lead to anti social reactions due to frustration about understanding on resolving these feeling. It is much more constructive to acknowledge these feelings, accept them as normal and share them with those we trust.

Getting in touch with, and understanding, your feelings is an essential part of achieving personal success in life. Sharing them with those we can truly trust is an added bonus.

In addition, successful people are not only able to get closely in touch with their own feelings, but are able to help others who may not have the skill, as yet.

Above all, accepting yourself, and where you are in life, and then working to improve yourself, using the personal goals you have set, is a key part of the success journey. Getting in touch with your feelings is an integral part of that process.

Get the right advice

We all like to buy the best. One of the problems with being constantly barraged with advertising is that there can be a reaction against doing what is the best thing to achieve success; making the decision to get good advice.

One particularly important example is personal investment. A friend told me recently that, by getting professional advice, he was able to get a much better return on his savings.

Do not worry about being barraged with advertising material. It is an essential part of knowing what is available, so that you can go out and make the best choice.

However, as with so many other things, the best referral is often a personal one. Usually this is brought about by you knowing that the particular adviser you choose has been successful in advising someone else that you trust and respect.

If you do not do this sort of reference checking, then you are just gambling on the providers own opinion about themselves and very few people in the selling business have a poor opinion about their products and services.

So, if you want to be successful in wealth creation, for example, get the right advice from someone that you know has created wealth for someone else.

Aim for someone that you respect as a self manager and decision maker - but don't fool yourself, the decision must be made by you. With such life critical decisions, such as finance, it always surprises me how many people still want someone else to make the decision for them. Do not let this be you. Get the best advice, but make the decision yourself.

Give of yourself

One of the things I have observed in people who are truly successful is their willingness and capacity to contribute freely to the welfare of others.

People who are successful are not normally selfish and do not keep their success strategies to themselves or avoid people who want to learn from their success On the other hand they are often humble and wonder what all the fuss is about.

On the contrary, they often are very open with what their approach has been and give freely of their time to people who want to know how they have achieved success.

Also, be aware these successful people do not charge for sharing , so I am not talking about the many 'Buy my system to become rich' programs that are advertised everywhere. I am talking about personal connections made at business events, and so on, where these people are often looking to learn more as well

This does not mean that they allow all sorts of people to waste their time. But in circumstances where it is appropriate, they are happy to speak about their strategies, usually to people who they can see are already making a real effort, and are on the right track.

Successful people usually have little time for people who are looking for the easy way out and are not prepared to do any of the hard work.

One of the benefits of being willing to share ideas with people who have similar goals is that you almost invariably learn as much from them as they learn from you.

So when you are on that path to success do not shun other people who are working for the same goals.

Take some time to share ideas, you will find that the benefit is mutual.

Giving compliments

An interesting area in life is the giving and receiving of compliments.

Accepting compliments is an acquired skill. Equally, developing the art of proficiently delivery a compliment is important and requires sincerity and inspiration.

A genuine, appreciative remark helps to reinforce our inherent self-worth (both of the giver and receiver) and is one of the best ways to develop good relations with other people.

The art of paying a compliment takes thought and practice. Many of us have experienced the discomfort of having a compliment fall through because we chose the wrong time or the wrong words. Choosing the right approach is just as important as choosing the right words.

Interestingly compliments are often offered publicly in a kidding fashion so they can be accepted without making demands of the recipient, who can laugh along with the crowd and happily accept the tribute.

However, genuine compliments are more powerful and the skill of speaking sincerely in tribute of another human being is a key skill for being successful.

Compliments, properly delivered and well received strengthen social interactions, help to boost the egos of both parties and encourage us to new achievements. Compliments are a powerful force for good will and a natural gesture used in the daily interactions of business people.

At the next level, successful teams build a culture based on mutual respect and complimenting one another on successes is a standard part of this culture. You can do this as part of your networking activities as well as part of your team building strategies when you become a leader, coach and mentor.

Go for perfection in something

One of things that I think is most notable about people who achieve success is their fascination with achieving perfection in at least one thing.

No matter how obscure the subject may be, successful people seem to choose to explore the limits of their abilities by trying to be the best or close to the best in a certain area.

The passion may not necessarily relate to their efforts to be personally successful, whether in work achievement, accumulation of wealth or their part time interest, but it does them give a perspective on what it means to achieve at the highest possible level.

Too often we think of the elements that make up a perfect performance only in terms of the most unusual and highly publicized events and individuals in the world.

In reality, we should all work to find an area in which to strive for perfection. It does not matter how small or obscure the goal. What matters is the process of aiming for perfection and achieving a really high standard.

The beauty of striving and succeeding in this way is the personal experience of total absorption in a subject on the one hand and, on the other hand, the flow on in terms of personal perspective with all other activities.

So whatever your passion, live it to the full. It can have an amazingly broad and meaningful impact on your life and can lead you to greater success in other areas.

Once experienced, the feeling of having done something really well remains with you and motivates you to excel in other areas.

Happiness In, Happiness Out (Hi Ho) Part One

So what is a quick way of getting positive brain food into your system to help you feel better and be more productive?

The computer industry have used a very effective acronym called GIGO (garbage in = garbage out) to capture the danger of assuming that a computer can automatically make sense out of nonsense.

Although the human brain is intellectually capable of producing sense from nonsense, emotionally it has much more difficulty.

The human brain copes much better, as does the computer interestingly enough, with a summarizing than a complete translation role. In other words, you'll always have some residual from the raw input to the human brain that comes out the other side.

Therefore, Hi Ho (happiness in = happiness out) makes a lot of sense. The more happy statements, visuals, musical sounds and feelings you can get going into the body the more happy feelings will be in there and the more likely it is that happiness will be the resultant effect in terms of output.

The beauty of this philosophy is that you do not have to take my word for it. Just try playing some music that you regard as very depressing and repeat to yourself some particularly negative thing about yourself and see whether you feel super happy. Do not do this for too long by the way because it is rather unnerving just how immediate the effect is.

Then, making sure you have it right on hand so you can counteract the negativity straight away, pull out some really happy music and repeat already prepared happy positive comments to yourself and just see the total contrast. You will see that using the Hi-Ho principle can help you keep your positive attitude as an essential part of your approach to life

Happiness In, Happiness Out (Hi Ho) Part Two

So how can the Happiness in-Happiness philosophy help in managing everyday situations, especially where other people want to transfer their unhappiness to you?

Well, that is the whole point of making HiHo a habit by working on it all the time. If you are not thinking about it all the time, you are actually letting your own HiHo (Happiness In = Happiness Out) turn into a GIGO (Garbage In = Garbage Out) from whatever hits you from negative people or the news media.

Because news and other media garbage, in particular, is not automatically translated into happy thoughts by the brain, it can give you a roller coaster ride that leaves you wondering why you are only happy for short periods of time and why that happiness is unpredictable.

It is amazing how easy it is to start understanding your unpredictable emotions if you monitor your inputs. You just need to be aware that, all too often, there is garbage going in to your mind that is uncontrolled, unpredictable and unwelcome.

Once you realize that you can intercept and qualify the garbage, it is amazing how you can lift your overall mood with the right sort of inputs as a substitute.

The bad news is that potential negative inputs are everywhere. The good news is that you can be on watch over your mood twenty four hours a day seven days a week and can always have the last say.

Finally, I have to say, this philosophy is not about living in a fantasy land. This is about realizing that bad news will always be there. It just has to be managed. However, without management it is a powerful enemy to your overall happiness.

Have a general liking for people

Working with someone who showed great care in his dealings with all the people in his organization reminded me, yet again, of the importance of a caring attitude.

This person was particularly focused and achieved his time and quality goals on a very large project, when many areas where he was dependent on others could have resulted in a failure.

Rather than becoming aggressive and pushing the other people into achieving their goals, he worked in a very caring way, got the best out of the people involved and organized a successful team effort.

When things get difficult, there is often a temptation to become aggressive and, verbally, bludgeon others into achieving goals that you think are the right ones. While this may work in the short term, it is very debilitating for the individual and the team in the medium and long term, not to mention completely wrong in so many other ways.

Getting a balance between achieving the immediate goal and developing the team for future challenges is an ability that should be developed as a matter of urgency.

One of the key factors in developing this style, and incorporating it into your personal success strategies, is to have a positive feeling about the work of others.

This is achieved by looking for their strengths, rather than allowing black clouds to form as a result of focusing on the inevitable weaknesses that we all have.

If you develop the skill of working with people's strengths and matching them with the right challenge, you'll find success in the short, medium and long term. The same principle applies to you.

Have a vision for life

So many people think that having a mission in life, or a personal vision, is the realm of one in a million people. On the contrary, it is something we all do and we all have.

Unfortunately, many of us miss out on the real pleasure of working with our visions and our achievements because we downplay how important they are in our lives.

Don't be embarrassed about your visions, luxuriate in them. A good way to start, of course, is to commit them to writing and get them more finely tuned. After this, you can share them with your family and your friends and test out their reaction to find out how likely they are to be allies in your quest.

The ultimate aspect of planning for success is to identify those people who accept that having a personal vision is a positive thing and want to work with you because they have similar views. Often, they are also looking to work with someone else, or at least communicate with someone, who is interested in achievement.

Although this all sounds really simple, do not be surprised to strike more than the odd person who thinks you are a little bit strange. This is because many people have been educated to be reactive rather than pro-active in life.

You may choose to take on the challenge of stimulating the interest of those who have not been involved in personal achievement before. Alternatively, you may find it more your style to only work with people with similar views to your own.

Whatever you choose to do, do not lose your own focus on having a life's vision about what you would like to achieve. Working towards your vision, into it and through it is a major personal success strategy.

Have that occasional blowout

In speaking to someone recently, I discovered that she had never really let her head go, particularly in her younger years, in terms of buying things she wanted. She had always been too committed to securing financial independence and stability.

As she grew older she became aware that there was a need to splash out and really be extravagant at times, to live life to the full. However, she had become so used to saving and scraping (which she did not like) that she could no longer enjoy the fruits of the prosperity she had achieved.

Naturally, we all define extravagance in our own way, but the impact can be equally beneficial for all of us.

You need to remember that life is a series of undulations.

The trick to being personally successful is to ride them like a surfboard or skiing down a slope, rather than being knocked over by the waves or rolling out of control after you have fallen off your skis.

Just like surfing and skiing requires a lot of practice, so does getting your life finely tuned. Yes, you have to swim out to catch the waves, and you have to have to do a lot of practice to be a good skier, but you do it so you can enjoy the ride.

There is no time like the present for enjoying the fruits of your work, so check out where you are on the slope or wave and either start paddling out or riding the wave, do not look in the wrong direction and get knocked over. A success perspective is one where you know what you value in life, work towards it and know how to enjoy it.

Once you are on top of a financial slope or wave and know you will not be breaking your neck or the bank, have a blow out. Buy that car, have that holiday, or whatever you have saved for. You earned it.

Help others

There have been numerous stories over the centuries about the merits and benefits of being charitable. Inevitably, truly charitable and caring human beings are honored and admired, often because this is the one thing they do not seek. Giving without the thought of reward is the only true giving.

I do not believe that there has been any change in this situation and it is still the case that to take the opportunity to help someone else, in whatever way, benefits not only the receiver but the giver.

There is a natural and positive part of our personality that allows us to benefit greatly from sharing with others. Whether it be our personal wealth, our knowledge or our personal energies in working with others on a charitable cause the process of giving has the capacity to enrich an individual's existence quite dramatically.

It is not just the feeling of helping that brings personal reward. Inevitably these activities allow you to relate to people who are similarly motivated. This feeling of camaraderie adds greatly to the basic experience of giving.

Those people who are truly successful know that the process of sharing brings them so much closer to a situation of total fulfillment and personal completeness. It is probably the one true indicator of our humanity.

Helping others does not work to a formula. Indeed, the more there is a formula, the less you are committing yourself. It is when helping others is spontaneous and personal that it gets right to the roots of who we are and what we believe about the meaning of life.

So when the opportunity arises don't hold back, give, in the knowledge that it is a natural and basic part of a successful lifestyle.

How far do you want to go?

Having spent my life assessing other people and attempting to help them realize their potential, one of the things that is most important to me is helping people understand that the rewards they feel are adjusted according to their circumstances.

Simply put, it is just as easy for an individual living a 'normal' life to feel pain and pleasure at the same level as individuals that may appear to be in much more privileged or worse circumstances.

I call this phenomenon the 'layers of life'. The 'layers of life' principle is extremely important when you consider your personal rewards and how they will affect you permanently or temporarily.

If we equate those layers arbitrarily with income (and I say arbitrarily because I do not want to be seen to equate success with money alone), the lower to middle layers represent most of us. We ebb and flow between an upper and lower level in terms of our ability to meet our financial commitments. We spend a bit too much, we save a little bit, we save a little bit more and then we spend too much again.

Throughout our lives, most of use are slowing rising through several layers to the point where we eventually retire and probably then drop back a layer or two in terms of the amount of money we have available to spend. This particular pattern of rising through the various layers of life is normal.

In terms of the layers of life, it is understanding just how far you want to go that is crucial to success. When you have set your goals and achieved them, be happy, do not look sideways and judge your life by what others have done.

The very old saying that comparisons are odious is one of the best known, but one of the hardest to live by, particularly when the modern media floods us with other peoples' stories. However, nothing changes the fact that you have one life to live, your own, and need to make the best of it.

Imagine life without a goal

I was discussing with my five year old son the value of dreams and why a child can perceive life as a never ending story. He grasped the idea immediately and quickly started to explain to his two year old brother about the value of imagining the possibilities that life brings.

In his case, it was imagining the acquisition of further stages of a particular toy building system that was popular at the time, but the example made me think of how sad it would be if anything that you dreamed of could be yours without effort.

A key part of success is having something to strive for, just as much as having achieved a goal.

It is indeed sad when you hear of people who do have everything (or so it seems) but in reality harbor a desire for normal things, while the normal seek fame and fortune.

More usually, normal people pursue normal predictable goals of happiness and certain material things, like a house and a regular holiday. In contrast, people who have all the material things possible and all their goals achieved, it seems, look for the most unusual success goals. They want to be left alone, be unrecognized in the street and generally live a normal life.

No being rich and famous does not necessarily make you miserable, but it certainly does not guarantee happiness. Life is unusual and unpredictabl3e and that is what makes it so much fun. It can be very interesting to think carefully of what this means about success for we average normal people.

We can use this knowledge to realize that, as a good friend of mine so often says, acknowledging the many others who said it previously and better, 'there is much more to running than coming first'. You need to enjoy the day to day and be grateful for its high points. We all have them and no one else's high should be allowed to make yours lower

In built work ethic

Many years ago, Psychologist Douglas McGregor developed a Theory X and Theory Y philosophy of management that became very popular. Basically, Theory X said that all people are lazy and do not want to work while Theory Y said that people want to work because it is a natural and enjoyable behavior.

Looking at this from a personal work ethic point of view, it is my view that people who wish to be personally successful will develop a Theory Y perspective, that is, they will see work as a productive activity that is enjoyable.

They will work towards a general philosophy of theory and practice that says that working is a good thing and one will not need to be coerced into working hard in a positive way.

There are two levels in this development of a sound work ethic. The first is the level where, especially by working with people of a similar philosophy, the individual will learn to perform well and be a good team member.

The second level is achieved when the individual has such a strong work ethic that, when combined with people who do not share the Theory Y philosophy of work, the person will be immune to the negative actions and statements of those who believe that work should only be completed as a last resort. Given the incredible power of peer group pressure, maintaining a personal philosophy of enjoying work can be difficult if you are surrounded by people who think the opposite.

Maintaining a personal philosophy of enjoying what you do, especially when those around you do not, is a major achievement. If you can do this, you will already have achieved a major personal success goal. You will never need motivation from others. You will be the motivator and a valued team member, when you find the right team.

Indispensability

One of the most important survival strategies in the process of being successful is probably one of the easiest to explain. However, most people have difficulty in appreciating its long term impact.

It is all about making yourself indispensable.

I have had many discussions with individuals and groups about the concept of making yourself replaceable in your job being such a good management principle. This usually sets all sorts of warning bells ringing for most people.

They are relieved to find out that the qualification that goes with this principle is that you should make yourself replaceable, certainly, but only in one particular job so that you can do a more important and interesting job.

Overall, it is very important that you make yourself as indispensable and irreplaceable as you possibly can, not only in certain situations but overall, by becoming recognized as an authority or an expert.

This does not mean becoming a self opinionated empty vessel. Being perceived as an expert, in a positive way, requires a lot of technical skill and the tactful use of strategic knowledge.

You have to acquire appropriate knowledge to meet your challenges and display it at critical times, but it requires really powerful communication skills. It is not enough to have the skill and knowledge, you have to know how to make it available and to the right people.

When you have done this, it is human nature that we stick with the people who are essential to us and you become a part of a winning team. So, for success, you must build your reputation as an indispensable resource and demonstrate the vital nature of your skills and knowledge, but you also need the right audience with the skill to act on your advice.

Intrinsic reward Part One

One of the most powerful ways of developing new behaviors is to set up an intrinsic reward loop. Basically, the best way to develop a permanent new behavior is for it to be rewarding in its own right and not on the basis of some future reward that it will bring.

If you are looking to achieve some major goal, a very good strategy is to identify one part of the path towards that goal that you will find immediately rewarding. If you can then establish that first behavior strongly in your overall life activities, you can start to bring other aspects of getting to the overall goal into the loop.

For example if your major goal is to get up every morning and walk for five miles, come back, have a leisurely breakfast and read the morning paper, but you find the thought of getting up early and exercising totally abhorrent, you need to find the element of that total behavior that will be most internally (intrinsically) rewarding.

It is most likely that having a leisurely breakfast and reading the paper will be most fun, at first. So, to work your way towards the bigger goal you should start by only getting up earlier and having the leisurely breakfast and reading the paper. Do no more in the way of heading towards your exercise goal until you have established the breakfast and newspaper routine so strongly that things just do not seem right unless you get up early each day.

Once you are up earlier each day, you can then stretch yourself to the next point of getting dressed and going outside to the area where you are going to exercise (if you are inside), and just sitting quietly and relaxing or just taking some deep breaths but restricting yourself to activities that are immediately rewarding. By just extending this process a little at a time, taking small enjoyable steps, you will get there, and are much less likely to fall back into old habits.

Intrinsic reward Part Two

In part one of this subject, I focused on establishing an exercise routine, something many of us find very hard. In part two, I want to elaborate on the general principles of applying intrinsic reward management to all activities.

You will recall that the basic principle was to take small steps that were immediately enjoyable and rewarding. In this way, as you work each phase of the intrinsically rewarding activities into your routine, it becomes more easy to move to the next phase. Fascinatingly, if you break for some reason from the routine to travel or whatever, it is amazing how the various reward patterns are retained separately and allow you to redevelop the total program much more quickly, when you are back to your usual routine.

Once again, the whole principle is centered on controlling your feedback to yourself. You need to be the one to design the program based on your knowledge of what you enjoy. By retaining total control over the reward process you get a double benefit.

First, the feeling of reward is that much greater when it is controlled by you. Second, the process is reinforced by your new ability to withstand the influence of outside events, which is that much greater because you have that much more control.

Now why isn't everybody doing this, so that there are no problems with obesity, giving up smoking, and so on. The secret lies in the power of peer group pressure and the media. No one is intentionally trying to do you harm, they just want you to be part of the crowd.

Unfortunately, this crowd is often not exercising, is addicted to sugar and fat and has a great time sharing these things with friends. It is very hard to order a healthy drink when the crowd is having something exotic. This is why the progressive acquisition of other habits that are resistant to this influence is so important. Small steps build a powerful habit.

It can work wonders

I was watching a team sporting event the other day. One team was leading the competition, while the other team was down towards the bottom of the competition ladder.

True to form, the more highly rated team beat the lower rated team convincingly. What I found fascinating about the encounter was the apparent similarity in the ability of the teams in the first ten minutes of the game. In fact, the lower rated team was leading after ten minutes.

For ten minutes, the lower rated team appeared to be playing more convincingly and as a better team than their opponents. However, after they had scored for the second time, and taken the lead, an amazing thing happened.

The lower rated team made four monumental blunders in quick succession. This allowed their opponents, who were losing, back into the game very quickly so that they gained control.

In making these major mistakes, it was almost as though the lower rated team could not mentally accept that they were beating one of the top teams in the competition.

They believed themselves to be inferior to the team that was playing against them and they performed accordingly. If you want to break out of a behavior pattern that is holding you back, you have to show a lot of confidence and commitment.

However, if you actually succeed in breaking through the barriers, you will overcome a quite severe self-imposed limitation and achieve long term success.

That it is not just ability, but attitude, that decides who wins and loses is not a revelation by a long way, but it is often forgotten in the heat of the moment, particularly when the contest is at its most critical point.

It is a moral thing

It was fascinating to see a friend, whom I greatly admire, get most excited in a discussion recently when we spoke about whether a person's talent could make up for them being a person of doubtful morals.

My friend was adamant that there was no way that he would ever accept that great skill, in business management for example, could make up for someone taking advantage of those who are less privileged.

It certainly reinforced my long held view that being successful and talented does not entitle a person to be beyond the law. Indeed, for successful people there is an obligation to lead the way in demonstrating the best possible corporate and personal behavior.

In pursuing personal success some people do lose the plot but, more often than not, the unacceptable behavior is not related directly to their career achievement. Nevertheless, these actions detract from the example they set.

In my view, striving for personal success goes beyond developing your own high standards. It involves setting a good example for others. So, quite apart from disapproving of unacceptable exploitive behavior, those who would be truly personally successful accept responsibility for showing others the way.

I see this as very much a part of my earnest friend's undisputed personal success. In his case, he not set a fine example, but he organized development training for those starting their career, with a strong emphasis on ethics and fair play.

What is so important about this example is that the individual involved is so competitive and still found plenty of time to share his skills and strategies for achieving success.

It is not magic

Communication has been talked about more than any other subject in the whole area of interpersonal relationships. Interestingly, all this talk appears to have contributed very little to improving the communications skills of the community.

One of the major difficulties that people have is their inability to get close to other people, in a not threatening way, and be honest about their feelings.

People who want to be successful work hard at developing the communication skills that so many people in our society lack. The secret to this skill is being genuinely interested in other people and their needs and realizing, and believing, that it is not all about you.

The ability to get close to people, to learn what they are really doing in their day to day activities and what they are seeking from life, is just basic communication, but it is amazing how few people can do this well.

This is not a magical activity, but it can feel like magic if you really connect properly with a person in an atmosphere of mutual understanding and respect. So how do you make this happen?

It merely requires taking the time to slow down, have a genuine interest in other people and realize that that general interest in others welfare is fulfilling in its own right.

So next time you suddenly feel yourself moving along at a ridiculous pace, not communicating and ignoring the feelings of others, just think about how much of life you are missing. Slow down, listen and live a little more through working closely with other people.

At a more philosophical level, you will be living life in a more positive way and helping to make the world a better place by creating a society that cares and shares.

Keep details

In a discussion with a senior executive, he commented to me that it is much better to have a blunt pencil than a sharp memory.

It is certainly a saying that I had not heard before and I thought I had heard most. What a terrific rule to go by. Too often we rely on our memory when it is just not up to the task.

One of the important things about being successful is knowing when it is necessary to keep yourself well organized in the area of taking notes for things that are to be done at some time in the future.

I recall several people that I have worked with who had different systems but essentially it amounted to making sure you do not rely on your memory.

One executive that comes to mind immediately had a writing pad that he carried with them in which he wrote everything that he needed to do and would methodically draw a thick black line through the item when it was completed.

Very old fashioned, I know, but nNot only did this person not forget what needed to be done, but that thick black line became a reward in itself as a sign of completion of the task.

I hear so often from people that time management is the one thing they just do not seem to be able to do well. This technique, using a blunt pencil, pen or whatever other implement is available to establish a permanent record of challenges that you think are worthwhile, is a great start.

Too often we procrastinate purely because we have not established a visible focus for the challenge ahead. So grab that blunt pencil from somewhere and get yourself a permanent place to record those challenges and you may find you have a simple system that will set you on the path to success, where more complicated systems have failed.

Keep people informed

So often you hear people say that they are unhappy with their work because they are kept in the dark and fed on bull dust.

It seems like such a small thing, but if you keep people informed you will quickly be recognized as someone who has the key to successfully working with people - individually and in groups.

People just hate to be kept in the dark. They do not want to know absolutely everything that goes on, but they do want to know about things that affect them.

So, in your day to day dealings with people, think about who needs to know about what. This is not as easy as it seems, because we all lead busy lives and are often finding it a challenge to be kept informed ourselves.

However, the problem we have in keeping ourselves informed is the solution to being a good communicator. Just communicate to others in exactly the same way you want to be informed. This approach will also make you more forgiving of others who are doing their best to communicate with you.

It may be members of your family, it may be other people that you work with, or it may be a community group. Whatever the circumstance, nobody likes to feel like an idiot, and there is no quicker way to feel like an idiot than to be unaware of something that everyone else assumes you know about.

If you want to be successful, you will quickly gain the skill of making sure that you tell people what is going on. Of course, like all skills, the more you use it, the better you get.

If you have this skill, people will respect you and want to work with you because you will have one of the essential communication skills for being a successful team worker, friend, organizer and manager of people.

Keep to your standards

When you are bombarded with other peoples' opinions on a regular basis, both in person and in the media, it is very difficult to do one of the things that is most significant for being personally successful.

For this reason, it is important that you set your own high standards in relation to personal behavior and stick to them.

After setting high standards for yourself it is so easy to compromise when you see other people taking it easy and working to a lower standard. Developing and maintaining a class act has never been easy and this is what sets apart the people who are truly successful in life.

The challenge is that you often have to set your own high standards and then maintain them in the face of a fairly heavy barrage of mediocrity. In addition, you need to do this without being singled out as a snob or know it all. The trick is to always take your work seriously, but be careful about taking yourself too seriously.

Another important issue is to keep your focus on the tasks you do and establish standards of performance that are unambiguous. This makes the job of setting future goals much easier.

Two ways of keeping your standards clearly in focus are to study the standards of people past and present that you admire and, secondly, to commit yourself to writing down observable aspects of your personal standards so that you can use them to check your performance at any given time.

In this way you can form your own rules to help you keep to the standard you want, rather than looking outward and being disappointed as you feel yourself slipping as a result of negative external influences.

You won't be disappointed when you set your own rules and follow your own high standards as long as you keep it real.

Know value

I was browsing in a used furniture store and spied a student's chair which was very familiar to me as I had seen it advertised many times at the local bulk furniture store.

It had always amazed me that chairs like this could be made and sold for $39.00 or less, representing such great value for the community. You can imagine my amazement when I checked the price on this particular second hand chair and found that it was listed at $40.00, a dollar more than its new price.

One of the most significant things all of us have to do in life is develop a real sense of two things from a commercial point of view - value and price. This was a classic case of something that was not a good price and definitely not good value.

Many people I meet are mini entrepreneurs when it comes to their own personal purchases and take a lot of trouble to ensure that they get a good price and good value. In their view, money is hard enough to come by, without frittering it away on so called bargains.

In our own way, all of us can be very successful in getting the best value for our dollar by just remaining alert and applying commonsense. In addition, the amount of media information to keep us informed is greater than ever.

Developing your sense of good value for money is a key part of being successful, not only because you save money but because it gives you such a feeling of satisfaction about the quality of your purchase as you use it and this flows on to your overall sense of contentment.

Another thing about buying quality is that it lasts and reduces the ever growing pile of junk that the human race seems to be dumping on the earth. So, by buying quality you not only enhance your self esteem and save money, you help save the planet.

Learn from the best

It may seem a little bit far fetched to some people, but I believe that all of us can greatly enhance our chances of achieving personal success by modeling ourselves on the best in the world.

I recall one friend who made a habit of reading the biographies of people he greatly admired and setting his own standards in terms of the best things that he read about these people.

Certainly, having our own core of ethics is the ultimate goal and we all have a set of behaviors to work with from the earliest age, but developing them and consciously improving them is something that too few people take the time to do.

It is amazing how many people believe that famous individuals throughout history were somehow magical. In fact they mostly had their feet firmly on the ground and achieved their reputations by practicing sound basic skills of interpersonal behavior that they learned from others.

Admiring the achievements of others and seeking to emulate them by applying their philosophies of effort and achievement in our own lives is one very valid technique for developing personal success.

This process is technically quite simple, because there are so many sources from which to get examples of greatness. However, the trick is applying the process in our everyday lives.

In this regard, it is important to remember that great achievement is not necessarily recognized worldwide, so be aware that your achievements are no less important for being local or family based.

There is a saying that if you aim for the stars, you might just land on the moon. The main point is that you have a go. Learn from and be inspired by the achievements of others, but pick you own goals and be satisfied with the effort and the achievement.

Learn the art of public speaking

A fear that is very high on the list of common problems for all people is the fear of public speaking. However, public speaking is an important part of your set of skills for being successful.

My experience is that many people get a healthy dose of the jitters when they are required to stand up in front of a group of people and do a presentation. There are some people how appear to love it, but many of these were once far less confident. The answer to getting confident was preparation and practice.

As with so many things, previous experience and preparation can take you a long way towards being successful in this area, but you have to get a start somewhere. So, where can you go to get started and learn how do you learn to speak with confidence

There are schools and clubs that specialize in education in public speaking at very reasonable cost. They teach you how to prepare and they give you the opportunity to practice with other people who want to learn exactly the same skills. These schools and clubs have been the starting point for many people.

Apart from formal preparation and practice, I believe the best way to start is to talk about something you know well and are passionate about. Some coaches start you off talking about a common item, such as a pencil, but I am of the view that the best subject to get you confident is one you know well. Either way, preparation and practice are what make perfect.

When fully prepared, you will be able to make confident presentations, explain your ideas and win others over to your way of thinking, because they will be impressed by your fluent and logical communication skills. So, if you still have more than the acceptable number of butterflies about doing public speaking, pick out a strategy that suits you best and become a confident presenter. It is a key area for self development.

Learning from others

One of the great attributes of people who are successful in all walks of life is their capacity to learn from others.

Even when giving advice or meeting with people in a teaching situation, successful people take the opportunity to learn from the experiences of others, no matter what those experiences might be.

The key attribute to achieving success from your interaction with other people is to develop listening skills. The big problem with listening is that you have to stop talking to take in information from other people. Many of us are so preoccupied with what we are going to say next that we tune out to what the other person is saying. However, really good listening skills are vital for learning and for general self-development.

When next in a conversation, try this little exercise. Without being too obvious about it, try to note how many times during a 30 second period you are actually thinking about what you are going to say next rather than paying full attention to what the other person is saying.

I think you'll be quite surprised at how self-centered you are with respect to focusing on getting your own ideas out rather than getting a full appreciation of the other person's ideas.

Follow up your interruption monitoring activity with some intensive listening by forgetting about having any ideas of your own momentarily and just expressing general interest in the ideas of the other person and what they mean to that person.

I think you will find that even these simple exercises will be a new experience that improves your listening skills. It tends to be a new experience for all of us. I hope you will also be pleasantly surprised at the benefits it brings in improving your understanding of people.

Listen to the successful

A friend of mine once told me that in playing golf you should never listen to the advice of anyone who had a handicap higher than 2. In other words, only take advice from someone who really knew how to play.

Looking to develop general strategies in life requires a similar attitude. Learn from and admire those people who have been successful and know what they are talking about.

There will never be a shortage of people happy to give you advice, but are they qualified to do so? What have they ever achieved that you would like to emulate? It's an acid test, but one that must be applied. Regrettably, it is applied very little and we all are inundated with advice of doubtful quality that tends to sneak up on us and influence us before we know where we are.

Successful people have the water off a ducks back technique developed perfectly and only open up and let the advice in when it is worthwhile because it comes from someone who is worth listening to. This philosophy is particularly important when looking at advice on investment.

Remember the old saying about looking out for people who say 'with my ideas and your money' we can both get rich. This is because working with these people is a recipe for disaster.

One of the key issues I discuss with clients who are planning a strategy after being retrenched from a job is to beware of people who are offering ways to invest my client's retrenchment payout in some golden opportunity. These people are not advisers or sales people they are opportunists.

Money is hard to earn and easy to spend and lose, so if you want to be successful, be a discerning listener, pick your advisers carefully and learn success from those who have succeeded.

Look brightly into the future

As I was standing waiting for a friend the other day, I saw a large group of high school students go by from the bus stop. It frightened me how there was a general lack of any chit chat and laughter. Their faces were generally stony, some looked terribly bitter and certainly their behavior was not at all consistent with the general perception that we live in a country that is still terribly lucky.

So why would these students have a cynical approach to life. I got some insight from a person I was speaking to a person who was recently working on a project involving confidence, self-esteem, motivation and goal setting for high school students.

She told me that the general training given in our schools does nothing whatever to increase the positive nature, general confidence or business entrepreneurship of students.

She felt that we needed to institutionalize issues such as confidence, self-esteem and motivation and so she was preparing a special human relations education course for high schools.

It is a concern when our society is such that we actually have to start school remedial work on young peoples' general attitudes to life? Nevertheless, if it is needed in the school program, any teaching of positive thinking, teamwork and achievement must be helpful.

Certainly, those people who would be successful will be those who do develop self-confidence, a good work and study attitude, set goals and guide themselves on to personal success, but it would be nice to see it as a first principle of schooling.

If our children do not look brightly into the future we have a reason to be concerned so we should take the lead and show them all the reasons to be positive and support any school programs that help them develop the life skills to be successful.

Managing money

We all have money difficulties at different times, but some people seem to have problems on a regular basis.

When counseling people in these situations, I use a very simple rule and try to have them accept it as one that they should learn to live by.

Basically, the money comes in and the money goes out. If the money that goes out exceeds the money that comes in, you are either broke already or are going to go broke.

Interestingly, there are a number of very large companies that could not live by this rule and went into bankruptcy. The principle is the same for individuals.

The wonderful thing for individuals is that they can take out a sheet of paper, draw a line down the centre, write 'in' on the top of the left hand side and 'out' on the top of the right hand side and list all the expenses and the income very simply.
If the 'out' exceeds the 'in', then some of the 'out' has to go.

If your affairs are complex, you may wish to consult a qualified financial planner, but for basic balancing of the budget the principle is simple.

'In' minus "out" has to be larger than zero for you to be viable in the long term.

An important part of this simple approach is the central role that you play. No one else can take responsibility for your finances without you having to sign away your legal rights and, fortunately, this is comparatively rare.

So, it is up to you to take the initiative and make the rules and live by them. Yes it is very hard, because we all want to have everything for ourselves and for our families, but this is unachievable for most people. Hence, skill of budgeting is vital for personal success.

Managing others

Although part of being successful is not allowing other people to manage you, unless you want to be managed, there is definitely a strong case for acquiring the skills of managing others.

Sayings like 'many hands make light work' are definitely true and if those many hands have a skilful manager then the work will be even more productive. Managing others does not take a degree in business management or psychology. It just requires sound commonsense about people having the same purpose and wanting to work together to achieve a goal.

Thereafter, the management of team activities is all about defining those goals well and organizing a plan and making sure it is followed to achieve those goals in the most efficient way.

There certainly are courses that you can attend to help you improve your natural management skills or books that you can buy but, by and large, commonsense and good communication is the key to successful management of group activities.

So, if you have an interest in leadership and you want to make it part of your success story, get into managing others. You will find that your enjoyment and productivity are greatly increased.

Just remember though, that you are not the only one who would like a leadership role and helping others to equal or better your achievements is the sign of a truly remarkable leader.

Unfortunately, leaders at all levels have great difficulty sharing power and this starts at the first level of supervision. You will be unusual, but most successful if you are able to build a team where the authority to act is always included with the responsibility for the outcome.

This is one of the most difficult and least achieved principles of success.

Mean what you say

An area that causes many of us frustration is having people say something that they do not mean or they do not follow through on.

A key factor in being personally successful is to say what you mean and to mean what you say.

If you establish a reputation for being straight forward and honest and following through on your commitments, you will find that people will come to you seeking your assistance and wanting to work with you.

So, be aware of what you are committing yourself to and that you do mean what you are saying and are prepared to stand by it. You will stand out among a mass of people who are happy to make grand statements but are not there to be counted when it matters.

One key point though is to resist the temptation to make everybody happy by never delivering bad news. Remember this is only a short term solution and will catch up with you in the end.

It is far better to be honest in the first place and deliver bad news, like not being able to attend a function or help a friend, in a straight forward honest way, and not make dishonest excuses. The people involved will be disappointed at first, but will respect your honesty.

One important aspect of this quality of speaking plainly with everyone's welfare in mind is the work performance or discipline interview. It amazes me how people cannot do this well, mostly because they fear how the person being disciplined will react. The person may not like what is discussed but, if you are fair and honest and allow them to respond, you will be respected for being honest and straightforward and making it a two-way conversation.

Remember, personal success comes from dealing with the issues up front and taking any associated pain honestly and openly.

Mental marking

One of things I try to do in defining things that are good for me and not good for me in the brain food department is to form a mental picture of each thing that comes forward, tick it, surround it with stars or put a big cross through it mentally. I sometimes use one of those modern symbols with a circle and a stroke through it to indicate that it is not allowed on this patch of brain.

I call this mental marking. It may sound all very humorous and even a bit trivial, but I find that keeping things out of your mind needs a few little tricks to prevent you falling into the traps. It is amazing how, just on a day to day basis, thoughts that you do not want to entertain will be disguised as things that you might be useful and you open up your brain.

It applies equally to that second piece of chocolate as well as doing something that is fun when you should do the work to meet that deadline. Mental marking is very easy really because all you have to do is form a suitable single image such as a book, a person, or a name and then just very firmly mentally put a large black cross through it or circle it and put a stroke through if it is not something that you want.

Hopefully, by having well defined happy message seeking devices operating you will have many more situations where you put up the same images and put a big tick next to them or surround them with stars to indicate how welcome they are into your thoughts.

Also, do not restrict this to external thoughts; it is also very useful for things that crop up in your own thinking. Do not forget an uncontrolled brain is a random firing brain that can put up all sorts of things, some of which will be negative. If you have this technique on hand, whether it comes from within you or without you, you will have your system organized for labeling, sorting and acting, according to whether things are positive or negative. It is yet another small technique for keeping those positive thoughts going.

Monitor your state of mind

We all have to be aware of the possibility that negative things around us will creep up on us and, before we know it, eat away at our positive attitudes and positive style.

Rationalization of sub-standard performance by comparing yourself constantly to those who accept lower levels of behavior is something we must all guard against. Without being too insular, it is important to be a self paced goal setter with standards that motivate you.

Sometimes it pays to be insular. I was at a function where the key note speaker called a physically impaired athlete a loser because he came second in an endurance race. We all knew he was trying to be sensational to earn his fee, but the audience was not impressed. This was a time to acknowledge that mostly the major competitor you have is yourself, and your personal best effort so far.

A handy little technique for making sure that your standards do not slip is keeping a diary of personal achievements as represented by long standing permanent changes in your personal situation or day to day behavior that you have worked for and achieved.

Referring to this list of achievements on a monthly basis helps you keep yourself on track in terms of never giving up any ground that you have gained, especially if you have slowed down a bit in your quest to break new ground.

It is not possible to do anything about change unless you know that change is happening. The same thing applies to monitoring your lifelong quest for personal success.

So, keep your record of achievements as proudly as if they were a world record, as they are more important to your personal success other world records will be. Set your standard and move up from there.

Networking

One phenomenon I have identified among highly successful people is their ability to draw on the widest possible range of experts to deal with any problems they encounter. They call on these experts fearlessly without any concern about being regarded as lacking personal knowledge of the area they are unable to handle or feeling the need to pretend they have it under control.

Quite the opposite, they see their real skill as being able to identify individuals who can help them solve these problems, rather than trying to developing the skills to so the detailed problem solving themselves.

So, a key skill in being successful is developing, at the earliest possible time, the widest and most useful range of contacts to form a network of support for every activity that you undertake. This applies equally in personal and in business undertakings.

An important aspect of this routine is the awareness that there is something in it for everyone. In this regard, the best people to have in your network are people who are building up a network for themselves.

These kindred spirits are aware of what is going on and will move more quickly and constructively to help you. Certainly, they will expect you to help them when they need it, but that will only enhance your own image as a performer, networker and contributor.

So whether it is a community project or a business venture, find the best people and swap skills and knowledge. You will find that two heads are better than one every time, provided they are the right heads.

In addition, looking at this challenge from a different angle, this is what good management and team building is about. When you are in the position to build a team, make sure you do not employ replicas of yourself or people who will not threaten your role. This is negative and short term thinking. Use the networking philosophy and add people that complement you and your team.

Network around your limitations

In business, the really successful people are those who have a network which consists of people who complement their skills.

In developing individual strategies for personal success, the same principles apply, even though the network may not be developed on such a formal basis.

The key issue for people who are successful is that they are able to fulfill their affiliative need, the need to be with other people and socialize, as well as their need for self-esteem, the need to be respected by others, through relationships which make them part of an informal team constructed to further the interests of the members.

Do not get me wrong, I am not advocating the shallow manipulation of others which is practiced by 'con merchants' who are in the habit of treating other people as objects to be used by them for their own gain.

The true personal network is all about the achievement of mutual benefit through complementary skills and interests which allows all the members to be more successful in the pursuit of their respective life goals. With the internet of course, there are networking sites of all sorts to join, but this does not change the underlying personal principle involved in successful networking. In fact, the speed and scope of the World Wide Web makes them more important.

You need to be genuine in your networking approach and hold true to the principle of mutual benefit. Modern communication, particularly the World Wide Web, has tempted many more people to enter the manipulative zone. Indeed, it has allowed this to be fined tuned in a gigantic virtual world with real life conaequences.

The immediacy of the new networks makes the fundamental principles even more important, but do not be scared off, because the technology also offers great opportunities for those with integrity.

Obsession

I have had the opportunity to work with a variety of very successful people and it has become clear to me that their success is attributable, to a very large extent, to an internal obsession or drive to succeed or perform to the best of their ability.

Certainly, they had other factors which affected just how successful they were, but they always had an inner drive which seemed to be beyond their control and drove them on.

Very often, this drive could be traced back to an event or events which started them on the road to proving their worth to themselves and to others.

If you do not have this inner drive, then being successful might need you to create an environment or situation where your level of drive is expanded, exaggerated or developed, (whatever word is most comfortable for you) so that you can achieve at the highest level that you set as your goal.

If you have to construct this goal framework it is important to remember that discontent occurs mostly when the equation 'effort equals results' is out of balance. A huge effort with little result brings the most discontent. Success through little effort is a different circumstance that brings a different sort of discontent or disillusionment.

Yes it is good to be innovative and efficient but this is different from manipulating the environment to give you extraordinary results without much effort. It sounds good, but it creates disillusionment and cynicism

Traditionally, the formula 'effort equals results' is best. It is well worthwhile keeping this in mind if you want to develop artificial motivators to get you up to that obsessive level of effort consistent with great success.

Openness to change

Constantly, there is change all around us. One of the worst aspects of change is having it creep up on you and take you by surprise.

Regularly, we hear of people losing their jobs, being transferred or having some other change happen to them which is totally beyond their control.

One of the important things in being successful is to be aware of the pace of change as it relates to you and working with it as an enjoyable challenge.

We all initiate change around us, regularly, and we do it with enthusiasm and commitment. What has to happen for successful management of external change is to apply the same principles of enthusiasm and commitment to externally imposed changes, at home, work, in the local community or on a national basis.

While the philosophy of 'if you can't beat them join them' is not always that palatable, the philosophy of joining with the majority vote and being a positive part of the change process has a lot going for it.

Also, if you do have to 'go with it, you will find yourself a lot better off if you have detailed information about what is happening, get involved in the process and do not ignore it until it is too late.

So, if change is there and inevitable, become part of it, get involved and you will find it is a much more positive process.

Alternatively, if the change is not for you, you might choose to leave the organization, club, country, or whatever, and try your luck elsewhere and an important part of personal success is making sure you have that option.

If after all this, you are stuck with an unpalatable situation, a positive attitude can still achieve a lot.

Peer group pressure

It is amazing how all of us are bound in some way by the limitations created by the opinions of others.

Indeed, so much has been written about the outcomes of peer group pressure because it can have devastating effects on individuals, groups and whole societies.

Nevertheless, the process of denying the power of negative peer group pressure starts with the ability of one person to resist negative influences on their behavior. Sadly, the worst of these influences are often enforced by threat of personal harm, both domestically, institutionally and globally.

The example used here is not so dramatic, but the limitation of personal freedom to achieve personal goals is the same no matter how and where it occurs. The key to this peer group pressure example is to assess when behaviors are not truly yours but result for making others happy, while making you unhappy.

I had the case where I was seeking to assist a young person to break away from pre-conceived ideas other people had placed in her mind about what they felt her she could achieve.

After several sessions she started to look outside those limitations and see a whole new world for herself. However, when she presented these new ideas to the people who were close to her they said 'that is not you, you are not like that, you are more like this'.

This upset her quite significantly. The incongruity between what she wanted to be and what people close to her wanted her to be caused her such stress that she went back to her old way of behaving. She returned to repeating in her mind the views that other people had about what she was really like and how she should behave. She took on their thoughts as her own.

The focus of the coaching was career choice, so the peer group pressure was nowhere near as dramatic as circumstances faced by clinical professionals, but the principle is the same and still results in a diminution of quality of life.

The individual was not acting in her own best interests, but in the interests of others and, thus, would not achieve her career goals, but the career goals others had set for her. Indeed, this is such a well known theme it often features in books and films.

At these times, it may seem difficult to find the true path to developing yourself without cutting off those who are important to you, if they will not support you. However, substituting other more supportive groups may not be the answer, and the loss of family and friends is a major life change that merits seeking professional advice.

Indeed, there are some horrendous stories about people who get in to all sorts of trouble following groups that promise to find them a new life, only to find they have less control in these groups than they had before with family and friends. One of the challenges for people who wish to be personally successful is finding out how to break away from those old habits that are sustained by the people who surround them, without totally dismantling all the good things they may have developed so far.

The trick is to ascertain which of the behaviors are really counterproductive, which are acceptable and can be worked on and which can be retained as part of the future you. The counterproductive behaviors have to be worked out of your life. The acceptable ones need to be shaped to become part of your continuing successful lifestyle. Finally, you need introduce new behaviors that are your own and not copied from your peers or accepted to make them happy. The key is to know which behaviors are being imposed on you and which you are choosing to 'impose' on yourself.

Physical fitness

There has been an encouraging trend for people generally to be more fit. Certainly there has been a strong trend towards taking early morning walks on a daily basis.

I mentioned this because it is a safe and inexpensive way of getting back into physical shape. Also, there is a lot of support for the view that a moderate amount of physical exercise is beneficial for everyone. The key issue is how to fit the appropriate exercise into a successful lifestyle.

Some people prefer to walk early in the morning. Others prefer to get involved with team sports. The attractiveness of the exercise is important, as it should motivate you to exercise every day or three or four times a week. The successful person will find a form of exercise that suits their physically needs and suits their temperament. This way they also avoid the biggest trap in the pursuit of health and physical fitness- making excuses about it 'not being my thing'.

Even some of the greatest champions have indicated that certain forms of exercise, which would be beneficial for their overall development, are just so boring that they do not persist with them.

So if you do attempt some form of physical fitness program, do not give up if the first effort is not rewarded. Look at other options and give other types of exercise a try. It is very likely you will find something that suits your schedule and your needs.

The reason there are so many different types of sport and recreation is because people have so many different interests. This is a big clue that you may have to look through a lot of option to find the one that will get you started and keep you on track.

No matter what you find to be suitable, the rewards will definitely be there in improved physical health and mental alertness.

Personal fitness matters

It was great to have a meeting recently with two people in their fifties who just brimmed with confidence and to see that a lot of it was attributable to their high level of physical fitness.

Both of these people had gone out of their way to keep themselves physically fit and as a result were mentally really on the ball.

Although it was only a sample of two, it really indicated to me that there is that ongoing relationship between keeping yourself physically active and your resultant capacity to remain mentally active.

Interestingly, one of these people saw the opportunity to go walking on a regular basis as his personal quiet time where he could plan future activities in a state of full mental alertness. He said that he felt he was getting double value out of his exercise program.

To me this double whammy of exercising and thinking was a wonderful example of remaining active for life and enjoying the benefits of exercise as it occurred. Certainly, this was one personal success strategy that was working well for the individual concerned.

The beauty of this relationship of physical fitness to mental fitness is that everyone can do it no matter what their state of health because fitness is a totally personal concept. Have fun look around at what you might be able to do and do not see it as work. You are in charge of this process, remember, so it has to be fun.

The range of options is enormous, so do not be put off if you do not find the perfect fit first time. In addition, keep the goal of getting a mental as well as physical benefit clearly in your mind when you are assessing the quality of your various exercise experiences.
So, get into the swing by doing a little to improve your physical fitness and then building your activity to a level where you feel it matches your need; your mental health and your confidence will be better as a result.

Personal rules and integrity

An area that I believe is problematic for our community is a general lack of personal integrity. I believe this has happened because so many people lack the opportunity to develop the skills needed for developing and living by their own personal rules in this area

Even with changing education systems placing greater emphasis on life skills, I believe the general core skills are lacking whereby people can develop positive rules for life. They need to learn principles that can be applied on a day-to-day basis for self improvement and improvement of the community, but the opportunity is just not there.

It is sad that so many people are not made aware, preferably very early in their educational experience, that learning core values can give their life such greatly added value. In addition, it can be such a simple and pleasurable task. As with everything, it is never too late to develop these skills. In essence, it only requires the most basic application of the following test. You just have to ask yourself the question - Which of your behaviors are in the interest of yourself, your immediate family and the community?

All of us answer these questions in different ways, and life is complex. If we truly apply the test, however, it is amazing how it can help us get focused. If we are honest and act on the results, the behaviors that develop all meet a similar standard of civil behavior and goal directedness that will carry us through the development of a successful lifestyle and personal career achievement plan.

One particularly challenging aspect of this process is the capacity of the brain to distort fact into opinion, and vice versa. You have to make sure you use observable behavior that would satisfy the test of scrutiny by someone else who did not share your values. So if you have not taken the time or had the opportunity think about it, sit down now and write down the values you live by and put them to the test.

Play the right music

Music is a very individual thing, as is the human voice and the human fingerprint. Music is also present in our daily lives on an escapable basis.

One thing we all know is that certain songs and tunes make us feel particularly good and, as we sing along, we remember the past and we associate songs with good things.

What many of us fail to recognize is that negative emotions can also be associated with music. This means is that the 'happiness in' component, which is so strong in some music, needs to be controlled.

Many people would say that they could define everyone's 'happiness in' with a musical formula. If this were so, there would not be the thousands of failures in the music industry for every single 'hit' that comes along. And the predictability of what constitutes a future 'hit' would not be such a hap hazard activity.

Fortunately, one of the big benefits of modern technology is the capacity to totally control your auditory environment in almost every circumstance. An added bonus is that controlling this auditory environment has a double whammy effect. This is because the actual involvement in the programming of your own auditory input can be so intrinsically rewarding and give you a still greater high because of the feeling of control over your inputs and outputs.

All that is required is a true and sensitive assessment of your own feelings in relation to the wide variety of auditory inputs that are available to you each day.

With a little extra sensitivity it is not too hard for you to identify how your feelings of negativity are associated with certain music or sounds and how your positive feelings are associated with other music and sounds and you can start to increase quickly the positives at the expense of the negatives.
Programming your mood does sound a bit weird, but it works.

Positive mental attitude

In terms of personal success many people just speak in a hyperactive way about always maintaining a positive mental attitude as though this will solve all problems.

In my view, having a positive mental attitude is very important but only as a facilitative component used in conjunction with carefully planned and implemented strategies.

The reason positive mental attitude gets so much attention is because its characteristic as a lubricating fluid on the machinery for achieving success is so critical. For this reason, I often tell people to think about positive mental attitude in exactly this way. If you do not lubricate machinery it very quickly starts to run poorly and then breaks down.

You should think of your personal success strategies in the same context. Your strategies and skills are the machinery and the positive mental attitude is the lubricant.

Thinking about positive mental attitude in this way makes it much more meaningful because it takes away the vagueness of where being positive fits into the whole picture of success.

Some people think that positive thinking is so strong that it actually substitutes for skill and hard work. That is not positive mental attitude, that is luck, which does exist of course but it has equal amounts of bad and good and is not part of good success plan.

A good success plan tries to eliminate the need for luck.
The key aspect of the lubricant analogy is the way it reinforces the need for an ongoing positive approach that supports the real determinants of success.

Forget the hype, just approach your challenges with the attitude that, if it is worth doing, it will be enjoyable, and you will find it will go well.

Pride

For many years people were fairly negative about anyone who could be described as proud. Images arose immediately of people who looked down on others and had a very inflated view of themselves.

These days, pride in work and achievement, and in sport and social activities, is something that is sadly lacking. The positive aspect about pride is that it has the capacity to drive you to set standards for yourself that allow you to achieve at outstanding levels.

Those people who can use the philosophy of 'take pride in what you do' in a positive way to reflect on the fulfilling aspects of what they achieve will have found a major motivator.

Pride is a terrific inwardly directed force for confirming appropriate behavior for achieving success.

So, if you are one of those people who have slackened off a little bit in the area of being proud of your achievements, get pride into perspective. You will find that it is both a reward for past achievements and a driving force towards further success.

A word of warning is needed here. It is in your hands to use pride in a positive way to build a positive image of your performance and your resulting success.

In this regard, just remember that the saying 'pride comes before a fall' is a warning that good pride is about internal motivation and bad pride is about thinking you are already there and taking your eye of the ball.

Pride and conceit are two entirely different constructs, but they often get confused. If you keep your eye on the prize, work to achieve what you want and retain an appropriate level of humility, you can be proud. You will also be in a position to make sure you do not become conceited and defeat the whole purpose of success.

Promote yourself

The Chief Executive Officer (CEO) of a very large organization, that I have had the opportunity to work with, always takes every opportunity to promote his company's product as the best in the world.

It is clear that any person could challenge this statement - and many do. When he makes this claim, however, onlookers and listeners understand that he boasts because he knows the impact it will have, not because he believes that he could argue successfully that his product was the best. This CEO knows that there are competitors who feel that their product is the best, but he knows how to use the skill of personal promotion and the blend of perception and reality to achieve his goals.

A critical personal lesson to be learned in being successful is to be careful not to present yourself in a totally boastful and shallow way because you will lose credibility. On the other hand, however, you should never overlook the great importance of presentation and the need to develop your image in a certain way to properly complement what you really have to offer.

We all have an image and we develop it for better or worse every time we go out, talk and interact with people. It is important to manage this process. If you know you are always on show you will do a better job of presenting yourself and building a positive image. Just make sure the image you are promoting matches the substance of who you are. It is when the presentation and the substance do not match, that we end up in all sorts of trouble.

If you want to be credible, you promote yourself and your product or service exactly as the CEO in this example. You make sure that people understand that you are working to achieve a credible business purpose, not just blowing hot air to make yourself sound important. Indeed, the more you try to sound important the less important you will become.

Protect yourself in negotiations

Dealing with strangers and negotiating and developing new opportunities are key skills to be developed if you wish to succeed. I often have the need to speak to people about what they really want out of a negotiation, what they really want in the way of a salary, or what they want for something they have got that someone else wants.

It never ceases to amaze me how loosely people are prepared to form agreements with other people whom they do not know at all. Certainly, there are times to take a chance, times to trust in a hand shake, a nod of the head, a friendship or whatever. Trust has an important place in the world.

However, there are also times, and they are much more frequent than people acknowledge, when you need to create legally binding agreements to ensure that you get what you deserve and what you have worked for.

It is extremely interesting that large corporations make contractual agreements to bind themselves on a regular basis and often have to resort to the use of those agreements to resolve their difficulties. This is because when individuals make agreements with large corporations, they more often than not give themselves none of the protection the large corporations insist upon for themselves.

Since the individual is outgunned in terms of money, resources, experience and everything else associated with winning any argument, it never ceases to astound me how little protection people give themselves against being on the losing end of business arrangement.

So when you enter into any serious agreement, have a careful think about getting it in writing. It may save a lot of heartache later. You may feel a little uncomfortable, particularly if you have come to like and trust the opposing party, but the term opposing exists for a reason. They are not on your side.

Read widely and be Informed

A particular characteristic of many people that are very successful is that they are widely read. I can hear you groaning now, but try to keep an open mind because I am not talking about dull and boring study.

Successful people take the opportunity to absorb as much information from all sources as they possibly can.

Also, they do not regurgitate this information in all sorts of inappropriate places. Rather, they use the information for their own planning and definitely not to try to impress others.

If you have not spent a lot of time reading books or absorbing information then it is best to start in a fairly mild way.

Take an interest in events in your community or take the opportunity to read more widely in your local newspaper or to find a community website. Just take the opportunity to develop an understanding of what is happening in the world.

When something really major is going on, take the trouble to get that extra bit of information, challenge yourself with the issues and think what you would do if you were the decision maker.

A well informed person is generally more successful and the more successful people there are the more successful the community will be. So try it, spread your interest areas just a little more, you will be surprised how the new information is both interesting and challenging, plus it will often be surprisingly relevant to your success journey.

Realizing your potential

I would like you to think about your potential and your performance. Potential is a function of both your knowledge and your attitude and your performance is a function of both your ability and your motivation.

When coaching people over the years, I constantly emphasized to them that their level of knowledge was one factor but their attitude about how they would use their knowledge was an equally important factor, sometimes much more important. They had to find the right balance.

In addition, to be successful, you should work towards achieving a balance between your potential as determined by your attitude and knowledge, and performance, determined by your motivation and ability.

Obviously, circumstances differ but the relative difference in influence of knowledge and attitude is not that great in determining your potential to achieve, and the same goes for motivation and ability in what you do eventually achieve.

In saying that performance is a function of both ability and motivation, I am emphasizing that ability is not the only factor which determines how successful a person will be, particularly in the long term. Motivation is absolutely critical.

So keep in mind that it is great to have ability but you need to be motivated to make good use of your skills and, how you prepare with your knowledge and attitude, the how you make a good start to the whole process of achieving success.

Recognize happiness

I recall conducting a program where I emphasized achieving on your own terms. During the first break after the session, I was approached by one of the participants. He was a fairly quiet man that had been pointed out to me by company management as one of the most successful non-management executives in the entire group.

This non-management tag was the key to his discussion with me. I had made the point in my session that it was not only acceptable but highly desirable to stay away from management responsibility if you knew you were successful in your chosen area and had no interest in pursuing a management career.

Apparently, until I said this, he had always felt like he had been a complete failure. Purely because he did not take a management role.

To me, that was just unthinkable. I certainly was pleased to have the opportunity to emphasize very strongly that, quite contrary to being a failure in any way, he was a major success, because he had been able to withstand the very strong pressures that are brought to bear on all successful operators to become managers.

This type of pressure is not limited to the push for management, it can occur in many different areas. Having people trying to change your attitudes, to make them happy with you on their terms, is another classic situation where you just have to avoid the pressure and make the decision for yourself that you are happy with how you are going.

Success in keeping your commitment to your own goals is critical to achieving fulfillment in life.

Rehearse your lines

So often hints about self-confidence are just so vague and do not really tell you anything other than you should be self-confident and it will be much better for you.

One of the things that I often tell people is the great benefit of mentally rehearsing what you will say in a difficult situation that you know is coming up.

Rehearsal or visualization means you need to imagine yourself in the upcoming situation and then say to yourself, or out loud if no one is around, exactly what you would like to say.

So often we all think about difficult situations where we did not say exactly what we would have liked. Later we think 'oh, if only I had thought of that'.

Rehearsing what you will say in a difficult situation that is coming up is how you overcome that feeling of regret of not being fully prepared.

So, if you know about a situation that is coming up that may be emotionally grueling, like asking for a pay rise or negotiating something difficult at work or with a family member, live the experience in your mind and practice what you want to say.

It may not go exactly the way you would like on the day but you will certainly be better prepared, and speak with much more self-confidence, than if you go in unprepared.

Like anything, interpersonal skills are developed by practice. A successful person puts in the time and effort to prepare.

Relationships

One of the major difficulties people have in being personally successful is in developing good relationships.

In my view, success in this area comes from developing the capacity to be honest with other people by reducing your fear of how they will react.

Most people tend to disguise or alter their presentation of, and their feelings about, a situation because they fear how the other person will react.

To be successful in this area it is important to do two things. Firstly, it is necessary to present your own impressions and feelings and desires in a straight forward and unemotional way. Clearly this is not easy, but starting with the more simple situations will give you some opportunity to develop the skill.

Secondly, it is important to understand and learn to cope with other peoples' reaction to an honest presentation of your feelings. However, this area comes with a 'proceed with caution' warning.

Do not just blurt out your feelings at the first opportunity. Work with very simple and unthreatening feelings till you develop the skill to ensure that the outcome is generally positive for both parties. Managed correctly it should be very positive indeed.

Above all, remember that none of this can work if you do not care about how they other person will react and makes sure you structure what you will say to them to make the situation as good as it can be in the circumstances.

Relaxation

One of the skills that escape many people is the ability to relax.

It is very simple really and requires no more than finding the time and place just to have a lie down and close your eyes.

It cannot be that simple you say, but, think about it, how often do you make the opportunity just to get away from it all?

When you are lying down, you can increase your relaxation by several simple techniques such as taking a few slow deep breaths and imagining yourself to be in a setting that you find totally relaxing. It may be at the beach or in the country, but it has to be a scene that makes you feel totally secure.

The trick is to use your imagination to the point where you can feel the cool country breeze or hear the sound of the waves lapping on the shore.

So make that five minutes or ten minutes to relax. You will be surprised how easy it is to at least partially recharge your batteries.

If you find this is something that works for you, can consider more advanced forms of relaxation. There are many yoga-based and other types of relaxation techniques. In fact it is a whole industry.

Of course, this all means nothing if you do not make the decision to give yourself a mental break.

Remain flexible to benefit from ideas

It is never appropriate to adopt the same strategy with different people, in any circumstance, because all people are different.

This was brought home to me very dramatically recently by working with two work experience students, one from high school and one from university.

The work experience student from the university indicated great interest and broad flexibility in approaching business challenges, while the high school student was quite shy and wanted to be involved only in a very limited way in the day to day activities of the business.

Interestingly, after allowing both students full opportunity to pursue their interests in their own ways, the outcomes were quite the reverse of what might have been expected.

The high school student made some highly significant suggestions on quite challenging projects, while the university student chose to adopt a much more narrow focus.

To me the important lesson for business managers is to never allow natural reticence, youth, or other factors or, on the other hand, confidence, energy and so on to influence your ideas about an individual's capacity to generate ideas and work as part of a team.

Just keep an open mind and always work towards dealing with ideas on their merits. The much discussed 'halo effect' and the 'emperor's new clothes' effect, where the true ability is disguised by undeserved hero worship, do not usually fool the successful individual. Be on the look-out just the same, they are alive and well.

Respect other peoples' time

A student told me recently of an incident whereby she was doing a project for a particular school. She had to attend a meeting at the school and was kept waiting for a very long time after the set appointment time had gone by.

She was quite unconcerned about this total lack of respect for the importance of her time. I personally thought it was a great insult and certainly something that any student of the philosophies of personal success would learn from.

Respecting the time of any individual is a key personal success ethic. Having respect for others and their rights is something we all should develop to the highest possible level.

Just because someone may be lower in the hierarchy does not mean that they have no rights and should be treated with less respect.

There are people who work brilliantly in reporting upwards and making a good impression whilst treating the people who work for them very poorly. I do not regard these people as successful.

Someone who is truly successful will manage up and down on the same basis. Certainly giving priority to more senior people whose time is more limited, but certainly not treating more junior people as having no rights at all.

For those who would be truly successful priority setting is never synonymous with a disrespectful attitude towards staff, suppliers, students or any other supposedly less important individual.

Respect the achievements and efforts of others

Inevitably, people who are truly personally successful will be those who genuinely respect the achievements and efforts of others in the community, at all levels, regardless of their level of influence or public recognition.

To me, this is because successful people respect all effort and achievement through an inner quality of empathy which allows them to be just that much more in touch with the world around them and the people that they meet.

This quality of empathy is one that is essential for personal success. To cruise or crash through life, treading on other people and bashing other people out of the way, has nothing whatever to do with personal success.

True personal success comes from working with people, enjoying that interaction and contributing to the success and fulfillment of others. So, have a look around you and see if you are able to appreciate what other people are contributing and achieving.

This can be a most illuminating test of whether or not you have an outward directed strategy that is consistent with personal success or, if you are selfishly inwardly directed and locked into a strategy of personal life being all about you.

True personal success is about being sharing and caring, not about being dominating and demanding. If you are already using this important personal success strategy, then you will know what I mean.

If you have not tried the caring and sharing approach to success, the good news is that it is never too late and there is no time like the present. So look around and find out where you can enhance you success by sharing your skills and positive attitude with like minded people.

Right first time

There certainly seems to have been a significant reduction in the use of the very old work theme of 'right first time'.

To me this makes this theme even more important, because with so few people actually practicing the 'right first time' philosophy it has that much more impact.

I recall working with someone who practiced this philosophy in every respect and I remember even now the impact that this person's work had on everyone concerned.

There is always the temptation to be just so daunted by the extra work required to get things right the first time, that you go with 'close enough is good enough'.

However, once you establish the habit and enjoy the rewards of a perfect performance it seems the fear disappears and the challenge becomes enjoyable and the outcome is truly fulfilling.

This right first time philosophy is a basic principle behind the Hints for Personal Success and Goal Achievement Psychoframes of Plan, Initiate, Innovate, Check, and Standardize.

When using the Check component of the Psychoframe for Goal Achievement, you make sure you accept responsibility, do the extra work, know and apply the standard and, own the end result. With this approach it is much easier to develop and maintain a right first time routine.

So, if you are looking to achieve personal success, work hard and practice the 'right first time' philosophy. The rewards will come to you immediately as well as in the long term as you develop a work method that will be the envy of those around you.

Rise above doing It tough

You know we all do it tough now and again. It is just the nature of life. The difference between people who do it tough as a habit and those who are successful is the development of the ability to take a helicopter view.

Often, mostly in business courses, I speak to supervisors and general managers about the need to understand that working with an organization in a senior position requires the individual to be able to visualize themselves hovering in a helicopter above the general fray.

This helicopter approach allows them to look forward and guide the organization to take advantage of the good ground or good water that lies ahead.

For individuals the same type of philosophy applies. When you are down there being buffeted by the big waves or you feel lost amongst the trees, it is hard to get a success perspective. You need to close your eyes, put yourself in your imaginary helicopter and rise up over those apparently uncontrollable activities. Then, you just look forward in time and space to where you <u>can</u> be if you pursue the right strategy.

Sometimes the helicopter view is enough in itself because you can see that the water or ground ahead is much more hospitable than where you are now. However, if the ground or sea ahead looks just as bad as your present location then you have got to do some serious thinking and take some serious action.

No matter what the outcome of looking ahead at least you have taken the initiative and do not feel lost and powerless where you are now. So, whenever the going gets tough, jump in your imaginary helicopter, rise up, look over your troubles and take a firm grip on strategies for the way ahead.

Routine can be good

Sometimes people become concerned about getting into a rut or being bored with their everyday routine. It is very important to understand that a routine can be a key part of a successful lifestyle

For one, just because things are done every day, every week or every year, does not mean they cannot be enjoyable. On the contrary, there can be a very strong feeling of contentment about the predictability that comes from having routine activities. Indeed, that can be a vital part of a successful lifestyle.

Secondly, the base that is built from a well ordered routine is the pattern against which more exciting events are compared. Without a benchmark life's high points would be lost amongst a host of accidental events.

So, just because we are creatures of habit, does not mean that those habits have to be regarded negatively. Quite the contrary, they form the basis for a successful and healthy lifestyle. It is all in your state of mind.

If you build the right routines and then set up your own high points you will be totally in control and I can assure you it will not be boring. The trick is to develop systems where you do these routine things more efficiently and leave yourself time for more creative aspects of your life.

Alternatively, as some people seem to do very successfully, you can multi-task and do the routine work with one part of your brain and be doing the planning or other creative work at the same time.

Just do not day dream around heavy machinery or the equivalent. Whatever approach you adopt, the important thing is to use your planning and positive approach to build a mixture of routine and excitement that suits your need for contentment as well as achievement.

Select your acquaintances

Snobbery is such a negative word for most people, but strangely it has a message for all of us, if only we would change the word to selectivity.

Selectivity is all about selecting the people you choose to associate with in order to ensure that you only get positive or constructive messages sent towards you.

This is not egotism in the sense of the positive messages being positive messages about you, but it is wholly geared towards maintaining a positive outlook by making sure that the things around you have a positive vibration. As I have said so many times, it is amazing how examples from nature can help us understand these phenomena.

For example, if you have a barrel full of apples and throw in one rotten apple, before very long the whole barrel of apples would be rotten. Similarly, it makes no difference if you have one rotten apple in the bottom of a barrel and fill the barrel with good apples, after a very short time, the barrel will still be full of rotten apples.

To me, this is nature's way of showing us that a small amount of negativity grows very quickly and is virtually unstoppable. So, if you want to avoid going rotten you have to keep company with good apples and develop the skills to recognize the rotten apples by the vibrations they give off. The best way to recognize these vibrations is that they will leave you feeling negative, drained and doubting yourself.

Good influences come from people who vibrate positive energy that makes you feel confident. Just try picking the good from the bad, it is not usually that hard, but do stay alert for situations where people are pretending to give off the good vibrations too get under your guard. .

Self image

One area where you have to be constantly alert to the effects of the eroding forces around you is your image of yourself or your associated self esteem.

I spoke to an apparently very confident woman who was pursuing a very successful career in the military. However, she recounted somewhat sadly her days of military training, where she, and other women, missed meals just to avoid the derisive comments of the male trainees.

In addition, she indicated an expectation that the same derisive comments would still be made at the time I spoke to her, many years after she had completed her training.

Why would such destructive behavior take place in an organization designed to develop confidence, leadership and teamwork. The answer of course, is the insecurity of the males involved, and their consequent use of a heavily developed negative female stereotype in an attempt to promote low self esteem and erode confidence.

This is a classic example of the need to maintain a positive self image in the face of lack of support from, supposedly, close colleagues. Too often in our society others will seek to reduce your self image, with the aim of offering you solutions that are for their own commercial gain, or in the case of these individuals, boost their own confidence.

There is so much of this behavior that developing and maintaining strong self-image and self esteem strategies to cope with negative input in work and social situations remains a key part of personal success.

While the strategies in this book are meant to help in these situations, they are not substitute for professional counseling or intervention when that is needed.

Self sufficiency

A key characteristic of many very successful people is their personal self sufficiency. That is, they do not feel the need to gain approval from other people for the activities that they undertake or how they manage them.

It is not that these people are anti-social by not liking people or by wanting to do things that are unconventional.

The key element is their belief in their own ideas and their lack of any need to have the approval or confirmation of others before proceeding with their own strategies.

This is a very simple concept to understand but a difficult one to implement if it does not come naturally.

There have been countless books written about this characteristic with authors setting out painstakingly the negative aspect of looking for other people's approval and thereby emphasizing the healthy nature of being your own counselor.

So if you are already a person who is prepared to go their own way in decision making and you mostly pick the right way, do not feel that there is anything negative about this characteristic.

The only thing that you may want to do is just liaise a little more with those around you to ensure that your independent decision making and action is not seen as a reflection upon them.

On the other hand, if you find it difficult to set and achieve goals and are constantly seeking reassurance from others, beyond the point of getting sensible advice, you may want to learn from the success of these independent thinkers and let others see your independent lifestyle for what it is - a choice to be self governing.

Set a good pattern early

Although I am very often approached by young people who wish to work on various projects and businesses that I supervise, I try to give as many of them as possible an opportunity to be involved.

I see one of the major benefits to them as the opportunity to demonstrate their reliability. Naturally, the response and demonstration of reliability varies tremendously.

I am still amazed, after all this time, at how initial enthusiasm wanes and some of the most enthusiastic young individuals turn out to be the least reliable.

This does not apply to just reliability. There are numerous characteristics that are easy to start with, but can decline quite quickly into bad habits.

One key factor in personal success is to not become a victim of the old saying 'that person promised so much but delivered so little'.

I have always said in business that you succeed by giving the customer more than they were expecting, the same holds true for personal success. Whatever you promise, make sure that you deliver more. You will be remembered and you will be much sought after.

The start of this process is listening and making sure you understand what the standards are, so that you can be sure to exceed them every time. Unfortunately, one swallow does not make a summer and you have to be persistent in your efforts if you want to have a real impact.

So, be persistent in setting high standards, be consistent about them being met and be consistent in the quality of your performance. The impact on your personal success will be dramatic.

Set small goals first

Over many years there have been endless conversations about motivation.

How do we get motivated? Despite this being one of the most studied areas of psychology, many people lack the motivation to make changes in some of the most important areas of their life, particularly their health.

Some small lessons have been learned, with the emphasis on the small. Certainly a technique that has been used most successfully by many people is to set small achievable goals and build up from there.

Proceeding in a step by step fashion, whether starting an exercise program, giving up smoking or trying to meet any sort of personal target, has worked for many people.

It is an interesting psychological phenomenon that, to be motivating for most people, goals have to be just the right distance away. If they are too far, or too close, people usually become de-motivated.

So, if you are having problems getting yourself motivated, have a look at the targets you are setting. They may just be too far away. Try to make them small bite size chunks and build on your successes. You will find yourself approaching that distant target much more rapidly than you expected.

The best part is that when you makes small steps a habit, you will find that no task it too big for you, because you know how to break it down into edible pieces.

None of this is new of course with sayings like the journey of a thousand miles starting with the first step, and so on, being so well known for a very good reason, its true. The key is making sure that first step is the right distance and in the right direction.

Setting an example

Recently a friend gave me a tremendous example of the impact of one very important strategy for personal success - setting a good example.

Apparently, he had been on a rain forest walk and on the way back had noticed an empty plastic drink container lying beside the track. Quite unobtrusively he had picked up the container and stored it in his bag and disposed of it later in a waste bin.

Unknown to my friend, he had been observed by a younger member of the group who shortly after, somewhat conspicuously, identified a piece of waste along the track, picked it up and took it along to a bin further on.

My friend went out of his way to compliment this young person in relation to their responsible attitude to the environment. Furthermore, he was delighted he told me later of the incident as an example of how much of an impact setting a good example can have in releasing the normally inhibited behavior of others in relation to socially responsible activities.

A keen awareness of the 'do as I do' thinking that influences not just young people but the general community is a key factor for personal success. Successful people realize that nothing they do goes unobserved and any negative things have the potential to cause deterioration in general community standards and any positive things they do have an equal capacity to influence things in a positive way.

Whether we realize it or not, we are all role models. Successful people do know this and do something with it. I can be as simple as having the courage to pick up trash when others don't or helping someone in need. The main aspect of this success characteristic is to do it because you want to and it feels right, even without and audience

Show creative flair

A fun aspect of working towards personal success is the use of creativity in your day to day activities.

We teach our children to be spontaneous and creative in their approach to their activities, hand making cards for the birthdays of their friends, writing short stories to tell their friends at school, but when it comes to ourselves we are the slaves of consumerism. We buy our birthday and Christmas cards and our stories and adventures all come second hand from a blitz of mega media.

Interestingly, successful people seem to have retained some of that creative flair and are able to instill it into their activities. They make that invitation to their personal or business function just that little more interesting, or relate a story in a really interesting way to a group of friends so that it is enjoyable, and so on.

Successful people care enough to put effort creative energy into their lives to make things more enjoyable for everybody.

If you have lost it, regaining your creative edge is not that difficult. It is amazing how easy it is to enroll 1 in a very basic course with some creative component such as drawing, painting or creative writing at very little expense.

Of course, it is not the creative activity itself that is the only benefit. It is meeting people who have similar thoughts, thereby allowing you to feel comfortable in once again expressing your creative skills.

So if you feel that life has taken on something of a boring veneer, break out, find some activities that are more creative, and rejuvenate your innovative side. You will find that the rub off is quick and highly enjoyable and can contribute a lot to your successful lifestyle.

Some day never comes

Many people promise themselves rewards in the future for working hard now. Unfortunately, many of them never follow through and give themselves the rewards they deserve.

I was speaking to a group at a function recently. One guest revealed to the group that he had always wanted to take an afternoon off to play golf and, some day, he was going to. I replied that, if that was what he wanted to do, he should do it now because 'some day' would never come.

If you have dreams of having a particular recreation or reward, you should plan to achieve that reward on a specific date. Do not dream about it in full awareness that you will never do it. That makes the dream a punishment for working hard.

Even if the dream is fun, the reality will be just that much more fulfilling. Also, planning to have your reward on a particular date should be part of your organized successful lifestyle.

For some people the effort of giving themselves the reward is greater than the effort that has gone into deserving the reward in the first place, because they just get into the habit of working all the time and forget that recreation is an important part of life.

Work and recreation balance is a big part of keeping yourself happy. Forgetting to maintain this balance in your life is easy to do because you forget just how rewarding and refreshing a proper break is compared to work, even if you have the greatest job in the world.

Don't let this happen to you. Do not fall into the trap of the 'some day' reward that never comes. If you've worked for it, take it and enjoy it when you want it. When you have had the break you will be that much more capable when you return to your work challenges.

Speed reading

Poor reading ability may be costing you time, money and even a better job. For most people today, reading is no longer relaxation. To keep up with the times we must all read newspapers, letters, bank statements, reports, promotional material, and on and on. Let us not even start to talk about email and the World Wide Web.

In getting a job or advancing in one, the ability to read and comprehend quickly can mean the difference between success and failure. Yet the unfortunate fact is that many of us are poor readers.

There is one common problem: the inability to 'shift gears' depending on the nature of the material to be read. If the subject matter is difficult, careful, deliberate reading is justified; when it is easy, we should zip through it.

To increase reading speed, whole phrases need to be grasped instead of individual words. Initially, speed reading may seem to allow for only superficial comprehension. Soon however, as speed increases, so will comprehension.

In fact, the reverse can be true - faster reading can actually improve comprehension. By concentrating on increasing our reading speed, we can actually improve our focus and attention skills.

The best way to improve your reading, of course, is to enroll in a speed reading course. However, if there is no course available or you cannot afford special training, you can improve your reading ability yourself by using any of a wide range of self teaching guides.

This is one area where the World Wide Web is a great help because there are a lot of people out there who are happy to share their knowledge and contribute to your success.
Bit a problem though, you may need to be able to speed read to get through all the information on speed reading, Just kidding.

Stick to your guns

One thing we all must learn to do if we want to be successful is to stick to our guns when we know we are on a good thing and are developing a good idea.

There are just too many people around who will happily criticize what someone else puts forward, even though they will never come forward with an idea of their own.

Sometimes it is a real battle to continue with your own ideas when these people are putting you down but, if you can stick with it, the rewards can be enormous.

It is important of course to realize the difference between people having a go at you and picking on your ideas and those situations where people are constructively trying to help you.

Sometimes even the most constructive criticism can hurt. A key attribute of successful people is that they can pick the knockers from the genuine helpers and work with the genuine helpers while cutting the knockers right out of the system altogether.

So the two strategies to be developed are first, have faith in yourself and your ideas and, second, work with people who will constructively criticize and help you develop your ideas and ignore the destructive people who have no interest in success, whether it be yours or their own.

Especially do not be fooled by the idea that people who talk loudest and with most confidence have the best ideas. Good ideas and support can come from anywhere.
Just look for the positives, loud or quiet, and learn to assess ideas on their merits, not on who presented them or how much fuss they made. Making a fuss so that people won't criticize is as old as the Emperor's new clothes, but it is alive and well.

Strategies for tough times

When times are tough, and they are tough almost everywhere at some time or another, a recurring surprise is the large number of people who fail to cope with the situation. One of the main reasons for this is their failure to have a strategy for these tough times.

We all know about the saying that our aim was to drain the swamp but now we are up to our armpits in alligators. The problem with the tough times is that you become so involved, that you just cannot take a realistic view of what is happening.

Yes, you can pay your professional advisors, but this is expensive and may not be feasible when you have a financial problem. Also, you may often need the sort of advice at these times that professionals may not be able to give, but for which another business owner is the perfect choice.

When times are tough and you need some honest advice may be the perfect time to use your network to bring in one of your friends or colleagues, as a 'consultant' so to speak, to give you a third party appraisal. When there are you and your 'consultant' facing the problem, the odds look a whole lot better, but choose carefully as you need to be sure the 'consultant' is someone skilled that you trust completely. But give them a chance to refuse, as it can also be a good way of losing a friend.

If you are able to accept constructive criticism and you have a friend or colleague who is prepared to help, this strategy can be excellent because someone who is removed from the problem can bring you a realistic assessment of strategies to get through these tough times.

The truly successful person has developed their network and has this strategy as a standby to help them make sure they don't lose touch with reality and are able to make a dispassionate attack on the problem in the company of a friend and guide.

Success = Ability x Effort

So often you hear people say that they just are not capable or do not have the ability to do a particular thing.

One of the important things to remember is that success is achieved through both ability and effort. Many times I have seen people succeed, where others with more ability have failed, purely because they were prepared to put in the effort.

On the other hand it is important to realize that there are situations where no amount of effort will allow you to succeed. We all strike situations like this, but you should never give up easily.

If you are in doubt about continuing with something, get someone who is an expert in the area to assess your ability, but make sure they really know what they are talking about.

Do not just take the easy way out and say 'it is too hard', you might find an expert in the area will encourage you to achieve what you think is impossible because they know you can do it.

Being successful is all about realizing the combination of effort and ability that is required to get the best result. Yes you can 'work smart' and be innovative, but even the most successful and innovative people will tell you it was still a lot of hard work.

The popular adage that success is '1% inspiration and 99% perspiration' is just as relevant now as it ever was. Just make sure that you are not perspiring on something that has no future whatsoever, because your 1% inspiration has put you on the wrong track.

If you can truly understand your strengths and weaknesses and then apply the right balance of ability and effort, you will get the success you are looking for and deserve.

Success at all levels

I was at the check out of a large retail chain and was lucky enough to witness a brief but effective lesson in entrepreneurship.

The customer service person operating the checkout continued working in a brisk pace while she conducted a very lively conversation with an elderly couple buying their weekly groceries.

She concluded the discussion by indicating that the husband's retirement hobby of renovating old furniture was of great interest to her. She said she had recently purchased a chair that was in serious need of renovation and that she would be a customer for the husband's services.

Like any good business couple, the wife promptly took the checkout operators name and contact details and another deal was set in motion. Upon turning to assist me the customer service person said 'that's what I love about check out, you can always find someone to help you out'.

It delighted me to see yet another example of entrepreneurship in action at the coal face. People who wish to be successful realize that their level in the big business chain is irrelevant to their chance to achieve personal success.

This was just another example that being a cog in the wheel does not mean that you are significant, but that you are a vital part of the fabric of society.

It was also a further demonstration of how we can all make our world a rewarding one, if we realize that comparisons are odious. Yes, you can use the success of other to inspire you, but it does not mean you have to be them.

Your goal should be to make the best of what you have in your own special way, just like this checkout entrepeneur. That is success.

Take a risk

So often we hear people speaking about finding a balance and harmony in their day to day activities. This is very good advice and one of the general principles of being successful. Very few people who have been successful, however, have done so without taking some personal risks. Nothing stupid, but definitely putting themselves out of their comfort zone.

It's important of course to emphasize that the advice here is towards a calculated risk. That is, prepare well for that financial commitment such as a rental property or share investment, but be prepared to get just a little bit nervous about some of the new things that you are doing.

Once again the risk need not necessarily be a financial one.
It may that you will take some personal risk like trying some new activity that you are not particularly good at, but have always wanted to do.

It might be a social challenge like introducing yourself to that person that you have had the opportunity to speak to for some time, but did not dare because you thought they would not be friendly towards you. Whatever the challenge, throw a little bit of zest into your life and take some risks, chances are your path to personal success will be more interesting and more fruitful as a result.

Once again, a small warning is in order. Do not take failure personally, except as a motivation to do better. You cannot expect to take risks without some failure. The trick is for the risk to be calculated and the failure to be anticipated, if it is a possibility, and managed if it happens.

Of course you do not set out to fail, but the only people who never fail are those who never do anything. I know, you've heard that before, but you have to admit it's a good one. So, have a go or you will never know, will you.

Take control (Part One)

Although I have interviewed thousands of people over the years, it still continues to amaze me how very basic questions like 'Where are you going from here?' and 'What would be your ideal next job if you could choose whatever job you would like?' causes people quite a lot of concern.

You know, it causes them concern because they have not thought about either of the questions as being their responsibility. They have always thought about the idea of personal development in terms of what is made available to them by other people.

One of the most important parts of being successful is getting yourself into the state of mind, and then into the situation, where you participate fully in all the decisions that affect you.

Do not have all the options decided for you by someone else.

If you decide to let someone else make those decisions for you that is entirely different from constantly being attuned to thinking that the options are limited, and that you have very little control.

You do not have very little control, you have all the control, and it is up to you to make sure that you maintain that control of your life.

Be self governing and you will find it is most rewarding. It just requires you to accept that you are the best person to make decisions about how your life should be managed.

That seems so simple, but it needs you to believe it before you can take control of your own future and success. Yes there will be the usual degree of hard work and disappointment, but there will also be lots of rewards, and you will own both.

In property terms, it is time to stop renting your life and start owning it.

Take control (Part Two)

In speaking to a young woman who was contemplating a career change, I was required to emphasize very strongly that she had to be sure that the feeling of dissatisfaction she had with her work was not related to some problem with her approach to the job.

She was working with a large organization where she had very good conditions and reasonable pay, but her supervisor no longer liked his job or the organization. As she explained to me, this made her job much less enjoyable than it had been, to the point where she wanted to go elsewhere. Her boss was not doing anything appropriate, like bully and so on, he just did not like his job and it showed in his attitude.

Despite the fact that it was quite clear that her situation had been created by having to work for a boss who had a very negative attitude, totally unrelated to her work performance or anything she had done, she still thought that some of the blame for feeling dissatisfied should rest with her.

As I explained to her, one of the key elements in achieving success is to understand quite clearly which factors are controllable by you and which factors are out of your control. In this case her boss's negativity was not something she could do anything about.

As this situation was essentially out of her control, and this had brought about the situation which was making her unhappy, she needed to <u>take</u> control, find a new job and regain her work satisfaction.

This was not a minor decision and part of trying to put up with the bad work situation was the unknown factors associated with finding a new job, but she knew she was putting off the inevitable need for change. So if you find yourself in similar circumstances do not <u>assume</u> that it is your fault. Just weigh up the situation, take control and get yourself on track.

Thoughtfulness

A pet hate of mine is people who drive along the road throwing small bits of rubbish out the window, particularly cigarette butts and cigarette packets.

Whoever coined the term, think globally act locally, was really onto a good thing. Just as large corporations have a public affairs and community responsibility; successful individuals are aware of their place in the community and treat their environment with respect in every way.

This littering example is just one pointed way of trying to show how habits can develop that form part of the bigger picture of not succeeding as a responsible member of the community. Such habits extend much more broadly and quickly into the treatment of one's neighbours, the relationship with one's family and all areas where the core of community commitment is tested.

This is an extremely interesting and important area because the irresponsible things are not necessarily illegal, but they are still negative. This leaves the decision squarely in the hands of the individual, as to where they place their interests compared to the interest of others around them.

An interesting test is to consider in the original example how you would feel if someone constantly threw cigarette butts, empty cigarette packets, or any other form of litter into into your garden or left it on your doorstep. I think you would see your perspective change dramatically.

Without wanting to stretch this example too much, it is not any different at a local, national or global level. You just have to think about treating other people the way you would like to be treated yourself. With respect, courtesy and acknowledgment of their rights to share the world on an equal basis.

Try to keep hypocrisy to a minimum

All of us are hypocrites at times and do not live by the rules that we preach. However, it does not mean that we cannot attempt to live by a philosophy whereby we try to minimize our hypocrisy.

Being a straight shooter and living by the rules is a tall order, but definitely a worthwhile goal. The next time you are on your soap box and preaching about a particular situation, try to be realistic in your assessment of your own behavior in this area. You may surprise yourself with your limited credibility.

A very telling test is to think of someone else who has done exactly the same things as you have done and think carefully about what opinion you have of them. This may give you quite a fright.

We all have a blind spot about ourselves. If we can reduce this blind spot, it may not have a major impact on our own feelings and behaviours immediately, but it can lead to much improved relations with others and useful feedback on our behavior.

The end result can be a more honest and effective communicative style with far fewer hypocritical actions and a good start on a more honest approach to life.

I know you are thinking that this cannot be you. Sorry, but everybody is hypocrite in some way. The key to being more successful is admitting it and trying to keep it to a minimum.

The best way to start is by writing down the best characteristics that you think define you and then list under those characteristics the things you have done recently that confirms that is who you are. You may get a surprise.

I was so impressed by this simple exercise that I turned it into a formal process and registered a trademark called the Psychoframe.

Use peer group pressure correctly

The example of a full barrel of good apples not being able to make a rotten apple good again is just a tremendous example of the role of peer group pressure in our everyday lives.

If you expressly want someone who shares your values, whether it is something really simple like an interest in physical fitness or more demanding like a passion for marathon running, then it is best if they have the values before they join.

Positive and supportive peer group pressure is great for motivating your team to success, but not appropriate for changing others who join without the necessary commitment.

Well structured transparent selection processes, that allow both sides to make a good decision, are the best way to make sure a new team member will see peer group standards and pressure to perform as the reason they joined.

Many people think that if sufficient peer group pressure is exerted that a new member will change their standards when they are brought into the group. My finding in general situations in the community and in business is quite the opposite. The need to think about modifying a new team member's behavior is usually the result of a poor selection process on either or both sides.

It is essential that peer group pressure is a managed process that focuses on motivation and fully involves the individual or group concerned. Do not be fooled, this is a delicate area that can quickly spiral out of control. If any member of the group feels uncomfortable about the process, you are on the wrong track.

However, as a team motivational tool, peer group pressure can work wonders in achieving success.

Use the media/feed the spirit

Many people say that the expansion of the media has contributed significantly to people losing control of the happiness component of their lives. I do not agree with this because I believe that the human mind has the most amazing capacity to control inputs if it wishes to do so.

The habits that we have in relation to accepting what other people tell us, particularly in relation to what we should accept as true, have been well developed for hundreds and probably thousands of years.

If we believe the details available to us in relation to the behavior of human beings thousands of years ago, we are very slow learners when it comes to the media, but in those days there was not a lot to choose from.

Modern media can provide an opportunity for you to select many happy inputs that can make your internal state and external output just that much more positive.

Obviously, the capacity for 'garbage in' remains the same, but that will never change. That is why the onus is on you to manage the 'garbage' that exists externally.

Fortunately, the skills you develop to analyze what you see and hear are going to be useful to you for as long as you live and they will just get better with practice.

The issue of living in a spiritual life, whether you have one, two or two hundred lives cannot go unaddressed in how you live from a day to day point of view.

The way I see it, if you do have two hundred lives then you have a spirit that you need to be working on right now because feeding that spirit happiness is going to be a habit that will be of benefit to you on such a longer term basis.

Use the media/feed the spirit (continued)

If, on the other hand, you only have one life, the same principle applies because you need to be getting as much out of this life as you possibly can by feeding that spirit as much happiness as you can possibly find.

To me the important argument in this whole exercise is the fact that it recognizes that human beings are spiritual beings. The issue that we are talking about here is that you must feed the spirit. One of the most potent arguments that I can find for getting into spiritual feeding is that it is absolutely free.

You can have a virtual, spiritual feeding frenzy and it does not cost you a cent. And quite the opposite of having a physical feeding frenzy, there are no negative after affects. Quite the contrary the positive after effects of feeding your spirit are amazingly long lasting.

Also, unlike physical feeding, you do not have to restrict yourself to three meals a day. You can just be eating spiritual food all the time. A well fed spirit does not get obese; it gets so fit it can almost fly.

So, enough positive talk about a spiritual feeding frenzy. How does it work? That is the beauty of the process. The mechanics are really simple, but important. You have to organize your use of the media so that you only listen to what you program and shut out miscellaneous.

Technically this is simple as I said, but think about how much uncontrolled information you take in each day, especially from the media and you will see what I mean.

As you will find, cutting out all unwanted television, radio, newspapers etc is not as really as easy it sounds. It will never be perfect, but just thinking about what you are hearing is the start of a process that you can develop as far as you want.

Use your strengths, improve your weaknesses

For many years, personal improvement strategists have preached the merits of listing your strengths and weaknesses. This can be a very sound philosophy, but it must be approached in the right way.

After you have a list your strengths and weaknesses, concentrate on the strengths first. This will give you a sound base to work from. Then you can work on improving your weaknesses.

If you adopt the reverse philosophy, which people often do, and develop an unhealthy emphasis on your weaknesses, you tend to forget about your strengths and you can be in real trouble.

I favor listing as many strong points as possible, but only identifying one particular weakness that you would like to work on. Also, make sure this weakness is particularly susceptible to intervention at the time.

That is, work on using your greatest strength to improve your least weakness. Do not try to fix your biggest weakness first that can come when it is the only one left. In this way you give yourself a better chance of maintaining a positive base to work from at all times and making the elimination of weaknesses more achievable.

One really good aspect of this routine is the way it transfers to so many other challenges. No matter what the challenge, if you get used to starting from a strong positive perspective, things that may have seemed daunting before can become more achievable, particularly if you progress from easiest to most difficult.

With practice, you get used to looking at the positives and it seems to make the negatives a little smaller. Plus, you get used to looking at the negatives and picking the one that is most easily eliminated.

Value your friends

One thing that seems to be a problem these days, especially in the hub-bub of hi-tech communication, is the establishment and maintenance of really good friendships.

High technology and information overload seems to have had a destabilizing effect on many people's emotions, particularly loyalty. There seem to be so many new friends, acquaintance really, that everybody counts their friends by the hundred.

This has a major downside, as being pushed from pillar to post by numerous media influences seems to have made people more prone to doubting the loyalty of even their best friends.

This is a great shame as one of the hallmarks of true friendship is loyalty and loss of friends and loyalty can have a major negative impact on you.

While unquestioning obedience is always potentially dangerous, unquestioning loyalty is much less so, although it still has its limits.

Nevertheless, loyalty is one of the essential ingredients for building working and social relationships that help successful people establish and progress a secure and positive lifestyle.

Strangely with all these new networks adding friends, it is even more important to think carefully about the people to whom you are totally loyal and you could honestly say show you an unshakeable attitude of positive support. You may well be disappointed at how few there are among all those acquaintances.

The good part of developing loyalty is that once the skills have been established in one or two relationships it seems easier to determine situations where loyalty is warranted and to expand the loyal network of friends that is so vital to overall success.

Walk tall

Many years ago there was a song with the words "walk tall look the world straight in the eye". It amazes me how many young people tend to walk in a slouched manner with their eye directed firmly at the ground. Also, they often have a similar downcast and pessimistic attitude.

Can one affect the other? Well I certainly believe that approaching life in a positive manner begins not just with physical fitness but with an alert style shown by an erect posture, a confident look and generally purposeful movement. By the way I should add that walking tall has nothing to do with your height, it is your mental approach. Just thought I better get that out there.

Walking tall and thinking tall go together and a successful approach to life has as much to do with your physical approach to people as well as your mental approach. Interestingly, I believe the capacity to walk tall flows backwards from thinking tall. If you do not have a positive approach it is often because you lack confidence in your ability to deal with the days challenges.

To improve in this area you have to psych yourself up and use your improved attitude to knock over some slightly bigger challenges, reinforcing the positive impact of a better overall approach, and move on from there. It is definitely not easy to do if you have been in the habit of slumping along and the road may be hard with a lot of disappointments, but persevere. Improvements in this area can be very rewarding and often snowball into a whole new approach to achieving personal success.

A critical aspect of this technique is realizing that the positive attitude is just a device that you control to keep you motivated to use your skills to achieve your chosen goals. It has not magical properties of its own.

Watch out for the great pretenders

It always astounds me how people just keep cropping up, who think that to be successful they must put themselves above and ahead of others.

An organization that my team works with on a regular basis had reason to call seeking some information. The person who called insisted on speaking to me and would not convey any details about what they wanted done.

If they had spoken to the subject matter expert in the business right away, instead of me, it would have been much easier to arrive at a solution quickly. Unfortunately, the person who called was much more concerned about maintaining their status in their own mind by dealing directly with me, than resolving the issue.

This type of behavior was not only totally disrespectful of the people in my team who had to the work and get a good result, but also stood in the way of us delivering timely customer service.

It is, unfortunately, the case that some people work on the principle that 'you should never let the real demands of the situation get in the way of keeping your ego intact'.

People with this sort of attitude are on the wrong track. True personal success is about getting self fulfilment by working at the right level, with the right people to get the right result.

Successful people respect everyone on the basis of who they are, what they contribute and their individuality. In particular, they do not let a sense of their own importance get in the way of achieving an efficient outcome.

I was taught this, by example, by one of the most successful people I have worked for, Sir Zelman Cowen.

What does it mean to have integrity

Because I speak so often about integrity as an essential part of personal success, people often ask me what I mean, exactly, by integrity. Very simply, I answer that integrity is all about honesty - honesty with yourself and honesty with others.

There is an old saying in relation to entertainment that you should never let the facts get in the way of a good story (it is also used in relation to reporting the news, but we won't go there). In other words, in telling a joke, embellishment is an essential part of being successful.

That may be appropriate for joke telling, but in the business of real life it is the people who do not let the facts get in the way of a good story who lack integrity.

So, it is very simple really. Having integrity means that you are not careless with the truth.

Relating this to your quest for personal success, it is vital to learn to face up to the bad news about yourself, and others, rather than changing the facts to fit the circumstances.

Do not pretend that you do not realize that society has rules that are as plain as the nose on everybody's face and that they are there for the basic business of being fair.

Denying the reality of what has happened and how you acted may be tempting, but it is the path of self deception and ensures you will not learn anything from the experience.

So, speak the truth, expect it from others and promote the value of relationships based on truth and honesty. Follow these very simple rules and you will be perceived as someone who is achieving personal success with integrity as a key element in your personal style.

What is success: revisited

Having spoken so much about personal success, I thought it might be appropriate to revisit what personal success really means.

I have said before that it is definitely not limited to factors associated with money or power or any of the other issues that I am sure so many people have used to define success in their minds.

Personal success is not a narrow concept. It operates across a broad band where people's wants and needs are matched against their efforts to achieve their goals.

The important thing about this very general definition of personal success is that the assessment of achievement is individual. Success is not a comparison of you against other people. It is you comparing your achievements against the standards you have set for yourself.

For this reason, personal success and the contentment that goes with it can be achieved by everyone. You just have to decide what it is that success means to you and achieve your goals.

Even if many of the factors behind setting your goals are out of your control, this can all be managed with a simple SWOTOS of looking at your Strengths and Weaknesses, considering the Opportunities and Threats to your plans and then setting Objectives and Strategies to achieve you goals.

The dynamics of the SWOTOS may change, but they remain personal to you and give you control of your success environment.

It is extremely important to understand that the personal contentment that you achieve is equally fulfilling to that achieved by the greatest people in history. They just happened to get more publicity.

Write your own resume

An exercise I often use, especially with people I am coaching in goal achievement, is writing your own resume. In this exercise I ask the person to look forward ten years and physically write the resume that they would like to be able to show others in ten years time.

This resume involves everything that one would normally find in a summary of your life to date, but chosen by the person involved as important them.

Some people choose to include classic biographical details such as their age at the future time, marital status, number of children, hobbies etc. while other focus more on details of their work history and related career achievements of what jobs they have done during the time.

Normally people come back to me looking for a starting point. This is because clues to the correct path ahead are obscured or invisible because they are looking or facing in the wrong direction.

I find that if I can get them to truly look ahead and visualize that end point, then they can face in that direction and see what has to be achieved to arrive at that end point.

The key to what may sound a bit like career day dreaming, is being able to be in the moment ten years ahead. If you know where you want to end up, you can more easily determine your starting point and path to arrive at your preferred destination. Your goals will have all sorts of stepping stones that you need to achieve along the way and you need to list these and when you will achieve them.

So, if you are into life and career planning get out that resume, which I know you will have up to date, and write it for a time ten years in the future. You will be pleased about what it tells you to do today to prepare for tomorrow.

You are your own image

There is a lot of talk in the area of personal development training about being only as successful as you dream you can be. Also, that you will be treated by others exactly as you expect to be, or as you indicate that you want to be.

I am always wary of going overboard with these types of strategies, but I do believe that there is quite some truth in the thought that if you present yourself as a doormat you will be walked on.

However, the reverse end of the spectrum of presenting yourself as a king or queen and then expecting to be being worshipped does not necessarily follow. Also, it is not much a strategy for true personal success.

I think there is more to be said for ensuring that you present yourself as a person who is aware of your own worth as a human being and thereby set a base line to ensure that you have a platform from which to build personal success.

Certainly, you can work to build an image of yourself as an achiever, but it will definitely take a lot more than just rhetoric lots of talk about how wonderful you are. Indeed, you are better off promising less and delivering more.

So for me, making sure you present yourself as someone who will not be trodden on is definitely a strategy to go with, but the going full on in the opposite direction is not necessarily a recipe for success. I would be very wary about your prospects if you following a strategy based on image building and dreams alone.

Success is an area where achievement by action rather than words is the order of the day. Yes you need to promote yourself, as I have said elsewhere, but first you need to have something worthwhile to promote. It is important the product, you, can deliver the goods that you are promoting.

Conclusion

I have found that the hints presented in this book have helped people more if they understand the basic principles of personal success that I use in personal coaching. The personal success principles that I recommend are to be positive, intense, independent, courageous and sincere.

Basically, I believe that being positive helps you because you are prepared to consider more options and take more calculated risks. I am not talking about physical risks or even financial risks. Let me give you the simplest example. When you are looking for a car park, your tendency is not to look for one closest to the front door of your destination because you assume they will all be gone.

If you are a positive thinker you are happy to accept that there probably will not be a car park right next to the front door, but you will still go and have a look and then take the one that is closest. Contrary to statements made by some writers about positive thinking, there is no magic in this and a car park does not materialize because you think positive. That sort of talk is just rubbish.

If you take a positive approach, however, you may put yourself in a position to take advantage of opportunities that others, who are less positive, may not bother to consider.

It may be helpful to think about the reverse effect. Have you ever noticed that when you're feeling a little low, and yes we all get that way, you just do not have the energy to face up to the hard decisions.

If you were to have a complete nervous breakdown, which I hope you never do, you would find that making even the smallest decision was extremely difficult. My view is that being positive just gives you that slight edge at the other end of the spectrum when facing common day-to-day problems, like finding a car park.

Intensity flows on from being positive. Here, I tend to use the classic example of how hard it is for some people to get on with any type of work, in other words get motivated, particularly when studying for exams. The key is to rush right in. What happens with this level of intensity is not normally that productive from a final output point of view, but it sure let's you know pretty quickly what you are up against. When you know how much there is to do, you also know you have to get on with the job - now.

If you procrastinate, you still end up finding out how much there is to do, but you leave yourself too little time to do anything about it. So, intensity is what it takes to get in there and face the problem. I should point out that being intense does not mean being aggressive, it means being eager, earnest, energetic and then diligent. The best use of your energy is bringing your intensity to the job in a controlled and effective way, not wasting it on unproductive anxiety and anger.

The independent characteristic is all about deciding for self what matters and pushing back the inevitable peer group pressure that you will encounter in all areas of your life. Being independent in your thinking opens up not just a direct path to your goals but immense satisfaction in following that path. At this is not easy, because society is just full of influential factors, particularly in the media, telling you how to live your life.

For this reason, it is important to understand that there are only two forms of communication, passing on of information and influencing others. It is the information that you are looking for, but without taking on the almost inevitable influencing component that tries to push you down a path that may suit others but not you.

The more skilful you become at collecting the information you need to make your decisions, the more obvious the various influencing components will become. Your independence will be enhanced by your ability to work with truthful information, not opinion that masquerades as information.

Courage is talked about in so many different ways and there are many forms of courage. Courage for personal success is about having the personal strength to work on when the odds, and opinions, are against you. It is pursuing your goals because you know what they mean to you.

I have worked with a range of entrepreneurs and all of them had to overcome enormous cynicism to be successful. And no, it was not their own cynicism, it was the cynicism of the many people were just not able to accept that these individuals had vision and were going to achieve great things. In particular, there can be a great deal of envy of people who are successful.

You will need courage, based on your positive approach, your intensity about the value of what you are doing and the strength of your ability to think independently, if you are to overcome a variety of obstacles to being successful

Finally, sincerity is about doing all of the other things for the right reasons. This is your philosophy of life. The reason that you do what you do.

Without a sincere philosophy that supports everything else you do in your campaign to be successful, the taste of success will not be sweet. In my view, a person who approaches their personal success goals with sincerity earns respect.

There are many people who are admired, emulating and honored, but not all are respected. Those that are not respected are brought down by a clear lack of sincerity in what they bring to their life and to the lives of others.

THE BASIC PRINCIPLES OF PERSONAL SUCCESS

Positive behavior gives the pleasure of discharging stored energy through achievement, and achievement leaves you with an after taste of satisfaction and self-respect.

Intense behavior, driven by positive thoughts, brings issues closer, removes ignorance, reduces fear and increases the capacity to act.

Independent mindedness confirms you as the focus of decision making, which makes you personally secure, able to stand firm and reject negative influences, leaving you feeling positive, powerful, satisfied and secure.

Courageous behavior is consistent with the fearless independence and sincerity that sustains a positive and intense approach to life.

Sincerity is the essence of personal success because of the feeling of fulfillment it gives you and the power that it injects into your actions.

ACTION REMINDERS

Remember to practice the following actions

- Always think positive.

- Live each moment to the full.

- Make up your own mind.

- Eliminate fear of fear itself.

- Know, and say, why you do what you do.

PERSONAL ACTION LIST
(Key words, actions & events to memorize, visualize and discuss)

Positive

Intense

Independent

Courageous

Sincere

Final notes for my personal success plan

Index

Endnotes

[1]   E Hubbard, *Elbert Hubbard's Scrap Book*, Wise & Co, New York, 1923, p. 75..

[2]   AM Colman (ed.), *A Dictionary of Psychology*, Oxford University Press, Oxford, 2009.